MAGNETIZE WILD SUCCESS
A MAGDALENE MAVERICK GUIDEBOOK

ROSE WILDER

Magnetize Wild Success: A Magdalene Maverick Guidebook
By Rose Wilder

Copyright © 2025 Rose Wilder. All rights reserved. No part of this book may be used or reproduced by any means, graphic, electronic, or mechanical, including photocopying, recording, taping, or by any information storage retrieval system without the written permission of the publisher except in the case of brief quotations embodied in critical articles and reviews.

Disclaimer
The information contained in this book is provided for educational and inspirational purposes only and is not intended as medical, psychological, or financial advice. The author and publisher are not licensed medical or financial professionals, and the content should not be used to diagnose, treat, cure, or prevent any medical condition or to replace professional medical care. Always seek the advice of your physician, qualified health provider, or financial advisor regarding any questions or concerns you may have.

Any examples of earnings, income, or financial results are illustrative only and do not represent a guarantee or promise of results. Your success depends on your own effort, experience, skills, and individual circumstances. No express or implied guarantees of financial or personal outcomes are made by the author or publisher. Because of the dynamic nature of the Internet, any web addresses or links contained in this book may have changed since publication and may no longer be valid.

The views expressed in this work are solely those of the author and do not necessarily reflect the views of the publisher, and the publisher hereby disclaims any responsibility for them.

Published by River Rose Press
River Rose Press is an imprint of Flower of Life Press
Jane S. Ashley, Publisher

www.riverrosepress.com
www.floweroflifepress.com

River Rose Press books may be ordered through booksellers or by contacting: support@floweroflifepress.com

Cover Design by Natasha Allan
Interior design by Jane S. Ashley

ISBN: 979-8-9987870-4-1

DEDICATION

To every wild-hearted woman who has felt too much, loved too deeply, and dared to dream beyond the boundaries others set for her: This is for you.

To those who have been told to dim their light, quiet their voice, and make themselves smaller: May these words ignite the remembrance and the flame of your magnificent power.

And to the luminous warriors, the women who have journeyed through the dark valleys of trauma, survived the storms of challenges, walked through the deserts of lack and scarcity, and emerged not just intact but radiant. You who have rebuilt yourselves from the ashes, seeing the luminous divine light on the other side of your deepest pain. A reminder that through your courageous healing, you heal not only yourselves, yet also support the healing of all those who came before you and all those who will come after. You saw and embraced the light all along, even when it was just a whisper in the darkness. Your resilience is a beacon, your transformation is medicine, your victory is our victory.

I see you. I honor you. I love you.

And to Mary Magdalene herself, the original wounded healer who transformed her deepest challenges into her greatest gifts, whose authentic radiance continues to guide revolutionary visionaries' hearts home to their own divine sovereignty. Thank you for showing us that our scars can become our stars, our wounds, our wisdom, our survival, our sacred service.

TO MARY MAGDALENE

Beloved Magdalene, first example among the Mavericks,

Thank you for showing us that true power flows from authenticity, not approval. That sacred service comes from overflow, not depletion. That magnetic presence emerges from embodiment, not performance. Your legacy lives on in every woman who chooses sovereignty over conformity, truth over popularity, and love over fear.

You have been my guide, my teacher, my celestial sister whispering courage into my heart during the darkest hours. This work is an offering to your memory and a continuation of your mission to awaken the divine feminine in all her glorious, rebellious, transformative power.

TO MY READERS

And finally, most importantly, to you, dear reader,

Thank you for having the courage to pick up this book, to question the status quo, to consider that there might be another way to live and love and build a business that honors your soul. Your willingness to embark on this journey means everything.

You are the reason this work exists. You are the wild-hearted women who refuse to be tamed, the faith-filled, spiritual revolutionaries who won't conform, the Magdalene Mavericks who dare to live authentically in an inauthentic world.

May these pages serve as both mirror and torch, reflecting back your own magnificent truth and illuminating the path forward into your most authentic, powerful, joyful expression.

No woman is an island, and this work stands as testament to the incredible community of souls who have lifted, supported, encouraged, and believed. To each name written here and to the countless others whose love has shaped this offering, my heart overflows with gratitude.

With infinite love and revolutionary recognition,

Rose

—**Rose Wilder, The Magdalene Maverick**

"I read the Magdalene Maverick and felt like I was reading through a true disciple of Mary Magdalene teachings. Rose was able to translate stories of Mary Magdalene and modernize it through the frequency of abundance and certainty. She reminded me multiple times to trust my inner guidance system, trust the feminine way of exchange and to value my gifts, my voice and my unique expression in business. She brought me back to life. All the 'maybe I should...' have been evaporated, dissolved and extinguished! It's like they don't even exist anymore and the only thing that's left is me trusting me and my 'limitations.' This should be a handbook in every priestess's medicine bag. To remind ourselves that our greatest currency is our love. Thank you Maverick Rose!"

—J Muenz, **Unmuted Creatrix, Spiritual Teacher + Humor Priestess**

"Omg this is Gold! Gold anointing oil! I absolutely love Magnetize Wild Success and it resonates deeply. As I read, I hear 'Yes! Yes!' The lovely ceremonies Rose added are so beautiful and perfect. She has spoken truth with clarity, understanding, and with the Deep LOVE she holds. Wisdom from the alabaster jar... the anointing of that precious oil is pouring over as I read. Thank you so much for allowing me to read this."

—Jessica Porter, **Sacred Heart Healing and Weaving Studio**

"Rose's words will touch the deepest parts of your remembrance; she gently guides and invites you to become fully anchored in your own knowing, your Divine expression and birth right as an abundant magnet of immaculate wealth, health, and prosperity. Her words are a warm hug welcoming you back into alignment with what was and is possible for each one of us. A revolutionary Maverick illuminating the way for those who are ready to say YES to their highest and most glorious expression. A blessed gift for this world and beyond."

—Natasha Allan, **Krystic Mystic Priestess of the Rose**

"Most often you seek mentors for your spiritual awakening or to support specific goals, but some mentors seek you, appearing at just the right threshold in your life. Rose Wilder is one of those rare guides. She finds a way to you. When you meet Rose you quickly learn that she carries the codes of the divine mother—wisdom, perseverance, vision, and nurturing—tender, yet unshakably grounded. As an Abundance Coach and Magdalene Priestess, she creates sacred spaces where you feel fully seen, deeply connected, and gently called back to your own inner wisdom. Rose is a connector in every sense, bridging women to their sacred gifts, weaving communities of belonging, being, and reminding us that our wholeness is never lost. In her presence, abundance stops being a distant dream and becomes a living reality, rooted in spiritual truth and embodied love. Since working with Rose, I've seen the fruits of my labor beginning to ripen and doors opening with ease. Abundance is her frequency and I'm so glad to be under her loving wings. Working with Rose feels like being welcomed home."

—*Lauren Kimberly Moore, Certified Spiritual Director and Feminine Embodiment Guide*

"This book offers a sacred invitation to honor your soul's wisdom in how to release your business into the world as an authentic expression of yourself in partnership with Divine Love. Rose speaks to all the angst and low-key anxiety I feel at times throughout my entrepreneurial journey, giving words to the deep knowing inside me that there must be a better, more authentic way to sustainably build my business that honors who I am. This book gives insight into how to build your business and live life abundantly without burnout. I highly recommend it for those desiring to sustainably thrive in business and life with grace, softness, and Divine Feminine flow."

—*Ame K., Encounter Yoga LLC*

"Meeting Rose was a divine appointment—though I didn't recognize it at the time. In truth, it was Rose who truly saw me. She recognized my sacred potential long before I could see myself clearly, lost in the sea of women hustling to prove their worth. Rose called me into her world, and with great care and unwavering vision, she held space for my unfolding. Rose became the midwife of that resurrection. She reminded me that what I offer is not a product, but a pathway. That I am here to facilitate journeys, not simply teach classes. She guided me to lead from a place of soul rather than strategy, to embody my calling rather than perform it. Letting go of hustle culture has been an act of sacred rebellion, one that continues to yield blessings: a regulated nervous system, aligned relationships, soul-deep communication, and the opening of true abundance. Rose didn't just mentor my business; she helped me remember who I was before the world told me who to be. And from that remembrance, everything has begun to bloom.

—**Ba Mery Sledge, Temple Guide of the Rebirth Mysteries**

"*Magnetize Wild Success* is a very encouraging and inspiring read—well done! I felt the essence of serenity in your words, an invitation to embrace a powerful softness... The client case studies and examples add a unique and fresh perspective on what it means to be in aligned divine business timing. Also, the story about Mary Magdalene at the Tomb was so powerful in the way it emphasizes discernment in trusting yourself. The teachings around shifting from linear goals to spiral emergence are a beautiful pathway to follow, as it's so easy to get caught up in the rigidity of pressure and timelines. I highly recommend this book for anyone who wants to be fully self-expressed and achieve success from a place of authentic and magnetic presence."

—**Lara Leyton Cathcart, Visionary and Author of Where is NoWhere Emily?**

"As I read these elegant words, which are easy to understand yet carry such profound wisdom, I could feel an activation happening within me. I could literally feel Mary Magdalene's golden abundance sprinkling into my heart before I even finished the first page. WOW! This book is such a blessing and a magical gift. I keep thinking about how many women, especially those who feel unworthy, who push themselves too hard, who are dealing with chronic illness or pain, or who are forced into doing things that do not feel right in their bodies, will be touched by this wisdom. I cannot wait to share it with my clients and my friends so it may land on their hearts and help them rise into a world where they can live authentically, speak their truth, and charge their worth without ever second-guessing. May the women of the world never forget that each of us carries a sacred gift to offer, and it does not need to be forced. We do not need to prove ourselves. If we can simply remember the magic within the words of this book, the world will become a better place."

—*Tara Jo Kadlec, Love Your Journey Inc, Founder*

"Wow! Oh Rose, this is such a wonderful gift to the world. What an honour it was to be able to preview it. So much medicine condensed into one stunning offering. Every word pinged in resonance and validated so much of what Mary Magdalene has brought into my awareness though I have difficulty articulating and explaining in a way to do it justice. I adored the lovely rituals offered to deepen into this Magdalene wisdom. I feel this is an invaluable tool for all women walking the way of love AND all women in general. You have such a gift for writing."

—*Amanda Doyle, Anam Cara ~ Spiritual Guide*

CONTENTS

The Seed: Magdalene Maverick—The Art of Achieving Wild Success Through Divine Love 1

Introduction 15

    Gateway 1: Sacred Worth
    The Foundation of Magdalene Success 21

    Gateway 2: Divine Timing
    Success in Sacred Rhythm 41

    Gateway 3: Authentic Power
    Truth as Your Business Force 57

    Gateway 4: Sacred Circle
    Creating Your Soul Business Community 73

    Gateway 5: Divine Flow
    Honoring Natural Business Rhythms 91

    Gateway 6: Sacred Service
    Giving Without Depletion 113

    Gateway 7: Magnetic Presence
    Becoming a Beacon of Divine Light 141

    Gateway 8: Your Sacred Invitation
    The Magdalene Maverick Revolution Begins NOW 175

Acknowledgments 185

About the Author 189

Sacred Gift 191

THE SEED

Magdalene Maverick—The Art of Achieving Wild Success Through Divine Love

"She who knows her worth changes the world with her presence."
—*Rose Wilder*

A Divine Invitation

As an abduction survivor, my relationship with trust, power, and divine guidance was forged in the crucible of darkness that few others have experienced. My miracle, and I choose that word intentionally, lies in how I emerged from those shadowed hours with an unbreakable bond to the holy family, especially Mary Magdalene and Yeshua. This connection hasn't merely aided my healing; it has transformed my entire understanding of success, purpose, and divine calling.

What emerged from those depths was an unshakable resilience, the nurturing presence of divine motherhood, and the untamed spirit of a maverick that now illuminates everything I create. And beloved sister, if these words have found their way to you in this sacred moment, know that our souls were meant to connect in this divine intersection of time and purpose.

You see, when life forces you to rebuild your entire sense of self from the ground up, you develop an extraordinary gift: pristine clarity about what truly matters amid the cacophony of "shoulds" that bombard us daily. And here's a truth that might make your wild heart dance: those conventional success formulas they're selling you—the endless hustle, the rise-and-grind mentality, the social media hamster wheel—your soul has known all along that there's another path entirely. I call this the "Magdalene Maverick" way.

Pulls chair closer and pats the seat beside her with a knowing smile.

Come closer, beloved. Let's speak heart-to-heart, priestess-to-priestess, about what professional success actually means when you're walking the Magdalene path. Because here is what I have discovered through my own journey and witnessed in countless sisters who've joined me: What the mainstream business world labels as our "weaknesses" or "limitations" are actually our most powerful gifts when illuminated by divine love and purpose.

Mary Magdalene, the Apostle to the Apostles, was the first to witness the risen Christ. Some dismissed her as delusional, yet she stood unwaveringly in her truth. Her direct experience superseded what others claimed was possible. And precious one, this is precisely the invitation I extend to you: a way of creating abundance that may seem utterly radical to the outside world, yet feels like returning home to your most authentic self.

The Sacred Rewiring of Success

Let me offer you something that I hope will feel like a warm embrace for your entrepreneurial soul:

Your sensitivity is not something to overcome, it's your most potent business superpower.

Your tears are not signs of weakness, they're alchemical waters of transformation.

Your yearning for deep connection isn't "inefficient," it's your greatest business asset.

Your inner knowing isn't secondary to expert advice, it's your primary divine compass.

Your boundaries aren't obstacles to growth—they're the sacred container for your abundance.

When you attune to your inner guidance as your sovereign advisor, you access wisdom that transcends what any external expert could provide. This intimate communion with your divine compass becomes your North Star, especially when navigating decisions about your soul's work. As you honor the boundaries that this inner wisdom reveals, you are not merely protecting your energy, you are creating the alchemical vessel where your greatest abundance is born. This sacred transmutation happens naturally when you place your own truth above all external voices, allowing your unique medicine to flow unobstructed into a world desperately waiting for it.

The Magdalene Business Revolution: Success on Sacred Terms

Do you know what sometimes makes me burst into laughter? Imagining Mary Magdalene confronted with modern business advice. Can you picture her scrolling through reels about "crushing your goals" or "10X-ing your income"? Winks knowingly. This woman who remained at the tomb when others fled, who proclaimed her truth when doubters scoffed, would surely remind us to honor our deepest knowing, even when conventional wisdom screams otherwise.

What I have discovered through years of Magdalene's mentorship is that authentic success bears little resemblance to the glossy images we're sold. My most profound business breakthrough? When I completely unplugged from all social media. Gasps dramatically. Yes, total business heresy, according to conventional wisdom! Yet here's what manifested...

I began prioritizing genuine soul connections, the kind where divine feminine wisdom flows freely between hearts. Each client interaction became a sacred ritual rather than a transaction. And contrary to what business "experts" predicted, my practice didn't merely survive; it flourished beyond my wildest dreams. Because here's the truth they don't teach in business school: your greatest power lies in being unapologetically, radiantly yourself.

Remember, precious one, that we are here to embody both human vulnerability and divine power simultaneously. Perfect in our exquisite imperfection.

Sister, here's what I wish someone had whispered to me years ago: every single quality that makes you feel "too much" for conventional spaces is actually your most magnetic gift in the marketplace of souls.

Your ability to sense energetic undercurrents? That's your divine client alignment system. Your expansive, compassionate heart? That's your unique value proposition. Your need for sacred rest and replenishment? There's your sustainable business model for generations of impact.

The Seven Sacred Principles of Magdalene Success

I am thrilled to share with you what I call the "Seven Sacred Principles for Magdalene Success." These guiding tenets emerged from years of deep communion with Magdalene wisdom and have completely transformed how I approach business and abundance.

1. Sacred Worth

This principle stirs my soul to its depths whenever I connect with it. Consider how Mary Magdalene stepped into her power as a spiritual teacher in her own right. In an era when women's testimony held no legal validity, she became known as the Apostle to the Apostles. She never diminished her spiritual authority or dimmed her radiance. When she taught, she did so with absolute conviction in her divine calling. When she spoke, she carried the certainty of one who knows her inherent value.

I have witnessed so many modern priestesses suffering today, undercharging, overgiving, apologizing for their rates, yet your gifts are just as sacred as Magdalene's. I learned this lesson through countless painful cycles of saying yes to discount requests until I was energetically bankrupt.

Now I understand: owning your worth isn't just for your benefit. It's about honoring the Magdalene lineage and divine feminine wisdom flowing through you. Just as Mary Magdalene stood firmly in her spiritual authority during a time of fierce patriarchal dominance, you too can stand unwavering in the value of your unique gifts, wisdom, and sacred work.

> "Yeshua and the ministry were supported by Mary Magdalene, whose resources were used to support Yeshua." (Inspired by Luke 8:2-3)

By embodying your worth, you illuminate the path for countless sisters waiting for permission to do the same. Your prosperity becomes a beacon showing what's possible.

2. Divine Timing

This principle revolutionized everything for me, beloved. Mary Magdalene embodied divine timing at its most profound: She awakened at the tomb while others slept and waited in darkness for the perfect moment of revelation. She neither rushed the resurrection nor forced the mystery. She simply showed up fully and remained present until sacred timing unfolded.

In my business, this has meant trusting the quiet seasons instead of panicking, honoring the divine "no" that precedes the sacred "yes." I have watched countless sisters strain and hustle themselves into exhaustion, but I have discovered that our greatest abundance arrives through divine patience, not forced action. It's about attuning to the sacred rhythms of creation, which yield all treasures in their perfect season. When I fully surrendered to divine timing, opportunities began flowing in ways I could never have engineered through strategic planning alone.

3. Authentic Power

Prepare yourself for this truth, magnificent one, because it will transform everything. Remember when Mary Magdalene stood unwavering in her testimony when no one, not even the other disciples, believed her account of the resurrection? That's authentic power. Not power over others, but power sourced from within. She didn't try to persuade, defend, or explain. She simply knew what she knew and spoke her truth calmly and confidently.

I have watched this principle work miracles in my business and with my clients. The magic manifests when we stop forcing our message into someone else's formula and instead, speak our individual truth. I still remember the first time I publicly challenged the "hustle harder" narrative; my hands trembled as I shared my message. But the response was overwhelming, countless women had been silently waiting for permission to create success differently.

The world doesn't merely need your voice, precious one. It needs your unique perspective, your particular way of seeing and being. Your truth isn't just a nice addition; it's essential medicine for this moment. When you summon the courage to speak your truth, just as Mary Magdalene did, your words become liberation for others.

4. Sacred Circle

Mary Magdalene existed within a sacred circle of connection, and so do you. You're here to forge soul-deep bonds through your work, not surface-level "networking," but profound connections that bring clarity and support to everyone they touch. When I stopped trying to reach "the masses" and instead nurtured my sacred circle, everything transformed. Your true community recognizes your heart; they celebrate your victories and hold space for your evolution.

5. Divine Flow

Oh, sister, this principle revolutionized my entire approach to business! Mary Magdalene understood divine flow intimately. She knew when to speak, when to hold silence, when to step forward, and when to retreat. In your business, this means honoring your natural rhythms. Some seasons call for vibrant expansion, while others require deep rooting and rest. Both are equally sacred, equally necessary for sustainable abundance.

6. Sacred Service

Consider how Mary Magdalene ministered from her abundance (Luke 8:3), offering her resources, presence, and influence in service to the greater vision. This principle teaches us to align our service with our soul's purpose. It's not about depleting yourself; it's about giving generously, without overgiving, so that your presence becomes a blessing everywhere you go. Your energy becomes naturally magnetic. I intuitively recognized this truth, yet earlier in my journey, I tried the conventional approach, the exhausting way. Now, I understand that our well-being isn't optional; it's the prerequisite for our greatest contribution.

7. Magnetic Presence

This final principle embodies living your truth so completely that your soul-aligned clients naturally gravitate toward you. Mary Magdalene didn't chase followers; she was so anchored in her truth that people were magnetized to her radiance. I have learned to embody both the divine feminine wisdom flowing through me and the divine masculine structure that brings vision into form.

All these principles emerged from my intimate communion with Magdalene wisdom and my own healing journey. They aren't mere business strategies; they are invitations to a completely new paradigm of abundance that honors the sacred calling within you.

*Gently squeezes your hand.

Why I Abandoned Hustle Culture (And Why You Might Consider It Too) wink wink

Here is the revolutionary truth: Authentic success is not defined by social media metrics or external validation; it blossoms when we follow our divine guidance rather than chasing approval from online business gurus.

Here is what my professional reality looks like now:

- Some weeks, I work 3 hours; others, I work 30.
- I take random weekdays off for sacred rest whenever my spirit requires it.
- My content emerges from divine inspiration, not contrived content calendars.
- I implicitly trust my intuition about client relationships.
- I have released comparison and impostor syndrome.
- I have reclaimed precious time that no amount of money could buy.
- I have cultivated abundant calm and inner peace that radiates through everything I create.

Do you know what brings me the greatest joy in my work? Witnessing spiritual sisters step into their full divine worth and abundance. Whether they're attending one of my "Seeds of Abundance" talks or experiencing profound transformation in our "Luminary Abundance" membership, or holding monthly temple space together in our Spiritual Practitioners membership, each journey is uniquely sacred and divinely orchestrated.

I have watched these teachings transform lives in countless ways as we explore Magdalene mysteries together, creating sustainable, soul-aligned practices. Through my high-touch work, I have witnessed extraordinary maverick spirits elevate their relationship with abundance, success, and freedom as they dismantle outdated paradigms while building lives and businesses aligned with their divine vision.

The most magical part? Once these teachings take root, I see my private clients, powerful spiritual leaders and change-makers, applying these principles to discover their unique expression of abundance. Celestial wisdom, after all, is Mary Magdalene's greatest teaching: that each of us carries a unique light, a particular medicine, and a different way of expressing timeless truths.

Divine Business Practices for the Modern Magdalene Maverick

You know what still brings tears of gratitude to my eyes? The way divine guidance arrives in the most unexpected moments.

Like when I was struggling with pricing my offerings, feeling those ancient unworthiness wounds resurfacing. One morning in meditation, I felt Mary Magdalene's presence so strongly it took my breath away. Suddenly, I remembered her alabaster jar and received a profound teaching that changed everything.

The Alabaster Jar Principle in Practice:

- Anoint your workspace with sacred intention each morning.
- Price your services from a place of inherent sacred worth.
- Create a transcendent experience for each client.
- Honor the energetic exchange in every transaction.

Let me share a story that illustrates this principle, beloved. Years ago, divine guidance prompted me to completely reimagine my client welcome process. Rather than standard automated emails, I created what I call "The Sacred Abundance Temple Welcome." New clients or alumni receive a beautifully curated package containing:

- A handwritten blessing note.
- A small vial of consecrated rose oil.
- A specially selected quartz crystal attuned to their energy.
- Sacred success rituals to support their journey.
- Fresh roses whenever possible!

Is it more investment than standard onboarding, closing, or promoting? Absolutely. Has it been worth it? Beyond measure. The miraculous connections, referrals, and transformations that have flowed from this practice have been nothing short of alchemical.

*Moves closer, takes your hands in hers.

Magdalene Money Mysteries and Your Sacred Abundance

Beloved visionary, let's illuminate a truth that Mary Magdalene embodied perfectly: spiritual power and material prosperity are divine partners, not opposing forces. While many modern spiritual leaders struggle with charging for their gifts, Mary Magdalene shows us another way.

Remember the alabaster jar containing precious spikenard? That sacred offering was worth an entire year's wages! Yet Mary Magdalene approached with absolute certainty in its value and purpose. She didn't diminish its worth. She didn't offer a discount. She simply knew the perfect alignment between spiritual offering and material value.

When you find yourself undercharging, overgiving, or caught in endless cycles of discounts and energy-draining exchanges, return to this powerful image. Envision Mary Magdalene standing in her truth, holding her valuable offering with complete confidence. This is your birthright, too, to know the worth of your spiritual gifts and to exchange them in perfect sacred balance.

Breaking the Poverty Vows

Let's address the magnificent elephant in the temple: the persistent myth that spiritual gifts must be given freely without fair exchange. Beloved, at some point, many of us unconsciously made what I call "poverty vows" in our spiritual work. We internalized false teachings about service and sacrifice.

Yet consider how Mary Magdalene actually lived:

- She was a woman of independent means and sovereign power.
- She funded Yeshua's ministry from her abundance.
- She possessed valuable sacred instruments and substances.
- She moved through the world freely, supported by her resources.

Pause and truly absorb this revelation. The woman closest to Yeshua, who understood his teachings most profoundly, wasn't living in lack or limitation; she embodied purposeful prosperity in service to her divine mission!

When we release our unconscious poverty vows and embrace sacred abundance, we honor the authentic Magdalene tradition. Take a moment to craft your own wealth vows, sacred promises to yourself that affirm your divine right to prosperity. Write from your heart: "I vow to receive abundance as my spiritual birthright," "I commit to honoring my gifts through aligned exchange," or "I promise to use my prosperity to amplify my sacred mission." These new commitments replace the unconscious poverty agreements that have limited your impact and well-being.

Whenever that old programming around charging for your gifts begins resurfacing, try this prayer, offered in deep communion with the Magdalene:

Prayer: The Blessing of Magdalene's Success

Our Beloved Magdalene,
Help me remember my sacred worth.
Let me receive as gracefully as I give.
May my prosperity be a light for others.
May my abundance create more good for all.
Thank you for showing me how to be both spiritual and prosperous,
Both in service and abundantly supported in return.
Guide us as we revolutionize success through divine love.
Strengthen us to trust our knowing,
Honor our worth,
And serve from our radiant overflow.
Let our work be a blessing,
Our success a beacon,
And our prosperity an ever-expanding blessing for all.
In divine love, so it is.

The Magdalene's Invitation to Your Wild Heart

This journey together has been so deliciously sacred, and now, beloved sister, as we complete our time together, I invite you into a powerful embodiment practice. Place one hand on your heart center and one hand on your sacred womb space. Breathe deeply into this connection and recognize you are the living continuation of Mary Magdalene's lineage in our time.

That wild, untamed, abundant maverick heart of yours that refuses to accept the conventional "shoulds" of success... that exquisite sensitivity someone once labeled "too much"... that profound longing for connection that transcends meaningless metrics... these are not burdens to overcome, they are your most potent superpowers.

You were called to this path for a divine purpose. The world needs your voice, your energy, your unique combination of gifts—the special medicine that only you can offer. And yes, you absolutely deserve to be compensated abundantly for sharing these sacred gifts! Hold fast to the alabaster jar, precious one, and remember the woman who knew her inestimable worth.

In those moments when the noise of conventional business advice becomes overwhelming, when you feel pulled to follow the crowd instead of your inner guidance, return to these Magdalene teachings. Light your sacred candle. Attune to your Magdalene wisdom. Listen to the gentle whispers of your soul. Your success doesn't need to mirror anyone else's. It only needs to resonate with your deepest truth.

You are not walking this path alone. Every time you stand in your worth, establish a sacred boundary, trust your divine timing, or choose depth over hustle, you walk in the footsteps of an ancient lineage of sacred maverick women who dared to forge a different path. And you journey alongside me and all your modern Magdalene sisters who are choosing this revolutionary way of being.

*Rises to embrace you with unconditional love.

Take these practices. Embody them. Make them uniquely yours. May they support you in creating success that feels like returning to your most authentic self. And remember, magnificent one: your sensitivity is your superpower, your depth is your differentiation, and the wisdom of your heart is your most trusted business advisor.

May your success illuminate the path for others. Let your abundance flow and bless our world.

You are witnessed, you are held, and you are so deeply loved. Until we meet again, let your light radiate without dimming.

With holy maverick love and rose-scented blessings, remember, beloved, we aren't merely building businesses; we're creating sacred vessels for divine love to flow through us into a world that desperately needs it. Every client connection, every offering, every expression of your gifts is an opportunity to emanate your light. You are blessed, and the Magdalene walks with you—always.

*Every woman who stands in her worth illuminates
the path for others to discover their own light.*

—Ancient Magdalene Teaching

INTRODUCTION

What is a Magdalene Maverick?

Beloved sister, a Magdalene Maverick is a divine revolutionary with wildfire in her heart and alabaster jar in hand, who dares to walk a radically different path to success, one illuminated by divine love rather than exhausting hustle.

She embodies Mary Magdalene's exquisite courage, standing unwavering in her spiritual authority even when the world attempts to dismiss her truth.

Winks knowingly.

Can you imagine Mary Magdalene scrolling through reels about "10x-ing your income," "killing it," or "crushing your goals"? This woman who remained at the tomb when others fled would surely remind us to honor our deepest knowing, even when conventional wisdom screams otherwise!

Can you just PICTURE it? Mary Magdalene with her thumb scrolling endlessly through social media posts about "dominating your niche" and Instagram stories promising to "hack your way to seven figures"?

This is the same radiant woman who broke open an entire year's wages worth of precious oil without a single thought about ROI or "maximizing her investment strategy." The woman who showed up at the tomb before dawn, not because some productivity guru told her that 5 AM was the "optimal time for manifestation" but because her SOUL called her there in divine timing.

Can you imagine her reaction to being told she needed to "build her personal brand" or "optimize her funnel"? This woman who walked in such authentic power that two thousand years later we are STILL talking about her magnetic presence? She didn't need a content calendar or engagement strategy, precious one. Her very BEING was the message. Her embodied truth was the marketing. Her unwavering commitment to her inner knowing was the strategy that outlasted every empire.

While the world obsesses over followers, metrics, crushing it, killing it, and dominating, our beloved Magdalene whispers a different invitation: "What if success could be as gentle as dawn breaking? As natural as roses blooming? As sustainable as the turning of the seasons?"

She understood what we have forgotten in our algorithm-obsessed world: True influence flows not from how loudly you shout but from how authentically you shine. Real abundance comes not from forcing outcomes but from trusting the divine orchestration of your purpose. Lasting impact happens not through aggressive tactics but through the quiet revolution of being so completely yourself that others remember who THEY truly are.

So while the business bros are busy "crushing" their goals, we Magdalene Mavericks are busy crushing the very NEED for those exhausting, soul-depleting approaches. Because honey, when you are aligned with divine flow, success doesn't require force... it requires FAITH. And that kind of success? It doesn't just change your bank account. It changes your very BEING. And THAT is the kind of revolution this world is dying for.

Because here is the beautiful truth she's whispering to every wild-hearted woman reading this: You don't need to kill anything to succeed, beloved. You need to resurrect the part of yourself that knows beyond all doubt that your authentic expression is the most magnetic force in the universe.

A Magdalene Maverick recognizes that every single quality that makes her feel "too much" for conventional spaces, her sensitivity, her tears, her yearning for soul-deep connection, her divine intuition, is not something to overcome but is her most magnetic superpower in the marketplace.

Introduction

She creates success on her own sacred terms, honoring divine timing over forced action, authentic power over external validation, and sacred worth over societal "shoulds." She knows that spiritual power and material prosperity are divine partners, most definitely not opposing forces, just as Mary Magdalene funded Yeshua's ministry from her abundance.

Most importantly, precious one, a Magdalene Maverick recognizes that her unique medicine, that exquisite combination of gifts only she can offer, is not just valuable, it is essential medicine for this moment. She stands in her worth like Mary Magdalene with her alabaster jar, knowing the inherent value of her offerings without diminishment or apology.

In essence, she is a holy maverick spirit who refuses to dim her radiance or follow conventional formulas, choosing instead to revolutionize success through ancient Magdalene wisdom and the untamed knowing of her own wild heart. And the world doesn't merely need her voice; it needs her particular way of seeing and being to illuminate the path for countless sisters waiting for permission to do the same.

A Sacred Confession Before We Begin

Beloved sister, I need to share something with you before we journey together through these gateways. As I have been writing this companion book, my own life has been walking me through deep initiations.

Professional challenges tested important boundaries that I have personally and professionally, the very ones that I teach about! Personal upheavals that forced me to practice divine timing when I wanted to control outcomes. Moments when my magnetic presence felt more like magnetic depletion. Days when sacred service felt like sacred struggle.

And you know what? This hasn't been a distraction from writing about the Magdalene way—it has been the most authentic research possible.

Every single principle in this book has been tested in the holy fire of real-time experience. Every gateway has not just been written but LIVED during one of the most transformative periods of my life. The wisdom here isn't theoretical. It's forged in the crucible of actual practice.

So when you read about standing in your worth while your very body and your world shake, or trusting divine timing when everything feels urgent, or maintaining sacred boundaries when life demands everything you have, know that these words come from lived experience. I am a woman who has been practicing these principles in real time, sometimes succeeding, sometimes stumbling, and sometimes falling flat on my face. Through it all, I always return to the Magdalene way as my north star.

This is what makes us true Magdalene Mavericks: not our perfection, but our willingness to keep returning to our truth, again and again, especially when it's hardest to remember.

GATEWAY 1

Sacred Worth—The Foundation of Magdalene Success

"Your worth is not something you create, it is something you remember."
—*Rose Wilder*

As I write this chapter on sacred worth, I find myself in the beautifully messy middle of my own worth journey, because here's the revolutionary truth that is not often talked about: even those of us who teach this work are still walking the path, still discovering new layers, still catching ourselves in the very patterns we help others transform.

Just yesterday (and I am sharing this with zero shame because authenticity is medicine), I caught myself almost apologizing for my rates to a potential client. The old conditioning crept in like fog, whispering those familiar lies: "Maybe you are asking too much… maybe you should make it easier for them… maybe you should give more."

*Insert record scratch moment here.

And last week? A trusted colleague, bless her for her loving truth-telling, pointed out that I was about to step into a place of massive overgiving. The very patterns I teach against! The irony was not lost on me, gorgeous. Here I was, about to pour myself out like water from a broken vessel, completely abandoning my own worth boundaries.

Gasp indeed!

Yet here is what I have learned, and what I want you to absorb into your very bones: Embodying our worth is not a destination we arrive at with a triumphant fanfare. It is a daily practice of returning home to our truth, a lifestyle, especially when life tests our resolve.

This is not failure, sister. This is being human while doing sacred work.

What transformed this potentially shame-spiral moment into pure gold was the awareness itself. I noticed. I caught the pattern. I saw the old programming trying to run the show, and instead of berating myself for "falling into an old pattern," I got curious.

The gift that emerged from this awareness? I realized these old worth-sabotaging behaviors arose during periods of exhaustion, when my energy reserves were low, my boundaries were thin, and my inner knowing was clouded by depletion.

Light bulb moment of epic proportions!

This revelation became my medicine: I now know to support myself with extra tenderness during these vulnerable times. I am setting new, loving, energetic guard rails in place, both personally and professionally, that protect my energy like a mama bear protects her cubs.

Because here is what Mary Magdalene knew that I am still learning: Our worth doesn't fluctuate based on our energy levels, our bank account, or our momentary lapses in confidence. It is constant, eternal, and inherent in our very existence.

Yet our ability to REMEMBER and EMBODY that worth? That requires daily devotion, conscious choice, and the radical self-compassion to keep coming back to our truth, again and again and again.

So if you are reading this thinking you should have your worth "figured out" by now, let me lovingly disrupt that myth. We are all works in progress, beautiful revolutionaries. The goal is not perfection, it's presence. It's the willingness to keep choosing our worth, keep honoring our value, keep returning to our truth even when the old stories try to seduce us back into smallness.

And that, precious soul, is where the real magic happens.

The Worth Revolution You Have Been Waiting For

Sister, I want you to imagine something that will SHAKE YOUR SOUL to its foundations and set your wild heart absolutely ON FIRE.

Picture yourself walking into a crowded marketplace, the ancient marketplace with Mary Magdalene, carrying an alabaster jar filled with precious spikenard oil worth an ENTIRE YEAR'S WAGES.

Feel the weight of that jar in your hands. Sense the precious resource contained within. Recognize the value you hold so casually, so confidently.

Now imagine, without hesitation, without apology, without a single MOMENT'S doubt about whether you should offer a discount or create a "payment plan special"...

You break that jar WIDE OPEN.

You pour out this precious resource with absolute certainty of its worth. You fill the entire room with its fragrance. You create a moment so profound it would be remembered for THOUSANDS of years.

THIS is the revolutionary act of Mary Magdalene with her alabaster jar—the most POWERFUL demonstration of sacred worth in spiritual history. And sister, it holds the key to everything you've been struggling with in your business, your relationships, and your divine calling.

Because what if, and I need you to really feel this in your very soul, what if you, my magnificent love, have been carrying an alabaster jar of your own all along, but you have been tiptoeing around with it, apologizing for having it, offering early-bird discounts on its contents, terrified to claim its full value?

What if your worth is not something you need to create, earn, hustle for, or prove through endless credentials... but something you simply need to REMEMBER?

The Magdalene Moment That Shattered Everything I Thought I Knew

Let me share something DEEPLY personal that revolutionized my understanding of worth and why, as an abduction survivor turned abundance priestess, I understand worth wounds in a way that cuts straight to the soul.

I was sitting across from a colleague that I admire, a brilliant colleague, a transformational speaker who literally helps people transform, watching tears stream down her face as she whispered, "But who would pay for me that much to speak on stages?"

And in that moment, something crystallized in me with such clarity it nearly knocked me breathless. You see, when you have had to rebuild your entire sense of worth from the ground up (like me following abduction) after someone tried to destroy it, you develop SUPERNATURAL clarity about what is real and what is conditioning.

That question does not come from your soul, beautiful one. That question does not come from your gifts. That question does not even come from YOUR lived experience.

That question comes from CENTURIES of systematic conditioning designed to keep women's wisdom accessible without appropriate honor. It comes from generations of feminine wisdom keepers who were burned, silenced, marginalized, and devalued. It comes from a world that has extracted women's care, healing, and nurturing while insisting it should be given freely, abundantly, without sacred exchange.

Let's name it boldly, because I have learned that naming our dragons is the first step to taming them:

The worth wound is not personal. It is ANCESTRAL.

Sacred Worth—The Foundation of Magdalene Success

Every time you:

- Undercharge for your sacred work because "people can't afford full price"
- Over-deliver until you are running on spiritual fumes
- Apologize for taking up economic space ("Sorry, but my rate is...")
- Discount your offerings when someone questions them
- Shrink your message to make it more accessible to everyone...

...you are not making a personal choice, precious one. You are living out an inherited pattern designed to keep feminine wisdom available without appropriate reverence.

But here is the MAGICAL truth that has the ability to liberate your entire existence: This does not require years of healing work or expensive therapy sessions. The moment you recognize that this wound is not actually YOURS, that it is a collective story you have been handed like a poisoned apple, something PROFOUND shifts in your energetic field.

Just as Mary Magdalene stood unwavering in her knowing of the value of her alabaster jar, YOU can stand in the sovereign certainty of your worth, breaking open old patterns that have contained your value for far too long.

The Divine Economics Revolution Your Soul Has Been Craving

Traditional business culture, that soul-crushing machine of endless hustle, tells you your worth is measured by:

- Hours sacrificed (work yourself to the bone, sister!)
- Credentials collected (more letters after your name equals more value!)
- Competition crushed (may the most aggressive entrepreneur win!)
- Followers amassed (visibility equals value, right?)
- Testimonials gathered (other people's approval validates your worth!)

But Mary Magdalene offers us a RADICALLY different model, one that has been hidden in plain sight for centuries, waiting for women just like you to reclaim it with both hands and a rebel heart.

The Magdalene Maverick measures worth by:

- The depth of presence you bring to every interaction
- The authenticity of your expression (no masks, no performance)
- The sacred intention behind your offering
- The transformational value your medicine creates
- The real lives touched over meaningless metrics

I still get delicious shivers when I remember the first time I quoted my first five-figure rate. My voice and my entire body was shaking like autumn leaves, I felt a bit like I might hyperventilate or pass out, my inner critic was SCREAMING, my ancestors were collectively gasping from beyond the veil, and I could feel my heart beating in my THROAT.

The client said *yes* without blinking. I still feel the happy sting of tears in my eyes at the memory.

Not because she was wealthy. Not because she was desperate. But because she could FEEL the certainty in my energy field. She could sense that I was not asking... I was OFFERING. Opening the field of abundance and opportunities.

In that moment, lightning-bolt clarity struck: She was not paying for my time, my credentials, or my strategic brilliance. She was investing in the TRANSFORMATION that only my specific energy signature and unique medicine can catalyze.

THAT is the exact ancient wisdom Mary Magdalene embodied with her alabaster jar. The jar was not valuable because of the hours it took to create, the credentials of its maker, or how it compared to other jars in the marketplace. It was valuable because of its ESSENCE and what it made possible.

Do you feel the REVOLUTIONARY implications of this truth vibrating through every cell of your being? When you recognize that your worth comes from the essence of who you are and the transformation your presence makes possible, you step outside the entire paradigm of comparison, competition, and credential-collecting.

You stop asking: "Am I qualified enough to charge this?" And start declaring: "This is the value of transformation I create."

You stop wondering: "Who am I to command this rate?" And start knowing: "This is the appropriate exchange for my medicine."

You stop apologizing: "I am sorry, but my rate is..." And start affirming: "The investment is $X, and here is the value and transformation that makes possible..."

The Worth Wound We All Inherited (and How to Heal It at the Root)

Let us get truly, COURAGEOUSLY real about where this worth wound comes from, because naming our shadows is the first step to transforming them into light.

For thousands of years, women's wisdom, gifts, and medicine have been:

- **Devalued** ("Women's work" consistently paid less across EVERY culture and century)
- **Appropriated** (Our practices stolen, repackaged, and sold by others for profit)
- **Extracted** (Our nurturing expected freely without reciprocal energy exchange)
- **Demonized** (Our discernment and intuitive gifts labeled dangerous, heretical, or "too much")
- **Commodified** (Our bodies and beauty valued above our minds and souls)

This is not some dusty historical concept collecting cobwebs in a university textbook. This shows up in concrete, practical ways in your business EVERY SINGLE DAY:

- When a potential client says, "That's too expensive," and you immediately doubt your rates instead of recognizing it as their worth wound speaking
- When you compare your pricing to others with half your wisdom but twice your social media followers
- When you extend sessions well beyond their sacred container because you're afraid of seeming "rigid" or "money-focused"
- When you add bonuses and extras to already-complete offerings because you fear they're not "enough"
- When you work with energy-draining clients because you are afraid to be "selective"

Each of these moments is not a personal failing, beloved. It is a direct manifestation of the ancestral worth wound that has been passed down through bloodlines and energetic fields like an invisible inheritance.

But here is where Mary Magdalene offers us such profound liberation, such STUNNING hope:

She walked into that room with her alabaster jar, in an era when women had virtually no economic power, in a culture that valued women primarily as property, and she BROKE OPEN that jar with sovereign certainty of its value. She poured out this precious resource without hesitation, negotiation, or apology. And when criticism came (because doesn't it ALWAYS when a woman stands firmly in her worth?), she didn't defend, explain, or justify.

She stood in silent, sovereign knowing of the value of both her offering and herself.

This, beloved Magdalene Maverick, is YOUR inheritance. This is your birthright. This is the frequency you get to embody every single day.

Breaking Open Your Own Alabaster Jar: The Sacred Revolution

When you set rates from that bone-deep knowing of your worth, pricing becomes a SPIRITUAL ACT. Your rates become a reflection of what you believe is possible for your clients, for yourself, and for the healing of our collective feminine worth wound.

Let me share a truth so STUNNING it transformed how I approach every aspect of my business:

Every time you undervalue your worth, you are not just limiting yourself. You are reinforcing the collective worth wounds for ALL women, especially those who will come after you.

Yet every time you stand firmly in your value with grace and certainty, you create energetic permission for countless others to do the same. You become a wayshower, a pattern-breaker, a sacred revolutionary in the economics of feminine wisdom.

Ask yourself these SOUL-STIRRING questions that will change everything:

1. What message does your pricing send about the value of feminine wisdom in this world?
2. What does it communicate about the worth of deep transformation?
3. What does it say about what is possible for your clients when they invest properly in themselves?
4. What does it declare about appropriate energy exchange for your unique medicine?

When you stand firmly in your worth with unwavering presence, you give others permission to value you properly. Your certainty becomes their clarity. Your sovereignty becomes their invitation to step into their own.

One of my clients raised her rates by 400% after an Alabaster Jar session. Know what happened? Her practice filled FASTER than ever before with clients who were more committed, more transformed, more grateful, and more in love with her work than any discounted client had ever been.

Why? Because energetically, she was declaring: "This work is sacred. This transformation is powerful. This creates profound change in the world."

And the universe responded with a resounding: "YES, IT IS."

The Magdalene Way of Sacred Access (Without Betraying Your Worth)

Now, I can hear some of your beautiful hearts thinking: "But Rose, what about accessibility? What about serving those who truly need my gifts but face financial challenges? Doesn't standing in my worth mean excluding people?"

Oh, precious sister. This is where Mary Magdalene offers us another layer of revolutionary wisdom. The Magdalene way is not about building walls or excluding souls who genuinely need your medicine. It's about creating thoughtful pathways that maintain the energy of sacred value while opening doors with intention.

Here are approaches that honor both accessibility AND your worth:

The Sacred Essence Offering:

Create a clearly defined, potent experience that delivers real transformation in a concentrated form. This isn't about diluting your work; it's about distilling its essence into a powerful first taste.

For example, I offer a 90-minute "Magdalene Worth Activation" group experience that addresses one specific challenge rather than my comprehensive mentorship. I price it at 20% of my signature offering—not as a discount, but as a complete experience with its own sacred value.

The key is being crystal clear about what this offering includes and what it doesn't. Present it not as a "budget option," instead as a specifically designed gateway with its own complete worth.

The Scholarship Exchange:

For those who deeply resonate with your work but truly cannot access your full rates, consider creating a limited number of spots where you offer adjusted investment combined with energetic exchange that honors both their needs and your worth.

This might look like: "In recognition of different life seasons we all move through, I reserve two spots annually for my mentorship at scholarship investment, combined with a service exchange that honors the full value of this transformation."

What makes these approaches different from simply devaluing your work?

Intention, clarity, and energetic boundaries.

These are not discounts given from fear or guilt; they are intentional offerings created from abundance and presented with complete confidence in their value.

Remember: Mary Magdalene did not apologize for her alabaster jar's worth or feel obligated to make it accessible to everyone in the marketplace. These pathways are offered from sovereign CHOICE, not obligation, and that energetic difference matters more than you can imagine.

The Alabaster Jar Worth Activation: Your Sacred Initiation

Set sacred space with rose petals scattered.

As I guide you through this sacred worth activation ceremony, I am holding space for my own tender places where worth wounds have surfaced during this writing process. Let's practice together, not as teacher and student, but as sister spirits walking this path hand in hand.

This powerful ceremony helps you embody the sovereign certainty of Mary Magdalene with her alabaster jar, activating your unshakable knowing of your sacred worth.

Sacred Intention: To reclaim and embody your inherent divine worth, releasing ancestral patterns of undervaluing feminine wisdom.

What You'll Need:

- A small jar or bottle (glass preferred, but any vessel with a lid)
- Essential oil of rose or spikenard (if available; any sacred oil will work)
- A white or gold candle
- Small pieces of paper and a beautiful pen
- Fresh rose petals (optional but powerful)
- A fireproof bowl for releasing

The Sacred Ceremony:

1. *Creating Your Temple Space*

- Light your candle, saying: *"I illuminate the truth of my inherent, unshakeable worth."*
- Place a drop of oil on your heart center: *"I anoint myself with the oil of sacred value, just as Mary Magdalene knew her worth beyond all questioning."*
- Take three deep breaths, feeling yourself settling into sacred presence

2. *Witnessing Your Worth Wounds*

On small pieces of paper, write specific ways you've diminished your worth:

- I apologize for my rates before stating them
- I give automatic discounts when asked
- I over-deliver until I'm spiritually depleted
- I compare my offerings to others and lower my prices
- I justify my worth instead of simply embodying it

For each paper, hold it to your heart, breathe deeply, and say: *"This pattern is not mine to carry forward. I release it with love back to the collective, where it can be transformed."*

Place each paper beside your candle safely.

3. Filling Your Alabaster Jar with Sacred Worth

- Hold your jar between your palms at your heart center
- Close your eyes and visualize Mary Magdalene standing before you, her alabaster jar glowing with divine light
- See her pouring the sacred essence of her jar into yours, infusing it with her sovereign certainty
- Feel this essence, liquid gold mixed with starlight, filling not just your jar but your entire being
- When your jar feels completely full of this sacred worth essence, place a drop of oil inside it, sealing the activation

4. The Revolutionary Worth Declaration—Standing tall with your jar held high like a chalice, declare with the voice of your most powerful self:

"I, [your name], stand in my full sacred worth as a Magdalene Maverick. Like Mary Magdalene with her alabaster jar, I know the immeasurable value of my offerings. I set my rates from divine knowing, not from fear or comparison. I receive abundance as my birthright and my spiritual inheritance. I recognize that owning my worth creates a sacred container for profound transformation. I honor my gifts by valuing them appropriately in the marketplace of souls. My worth is not something I create through achievements, it is something I remember from Source. I am worthy because I exist. My work is valuable because it transforms lives. My medicine is needed because souls are calling for it. And so it is, and so it shall be."

5. The Sacred Breaking of Old Patterns

- Take the papers with worth wounds and safely burn them in your fireproof bowl (or tear them mindfully if burning is not possible)
- As they transform, say: *"As Mary Magdalene broke open her alabaster jar, I break open the patterns that have contained my worth. What was limitation now becomes liberation."*

6. Sealing Your Worth Activation

- Place one drop of oil from your jar on your third eye: "My perception aligns with my sacred worth."
- One drop on your throat: "My voice carries the vibration of my value."
- One drop on your heart: "My heart knows its immeasurable worth."
- Place your jar on your altar or workspace as a daily reminder

Your Divine Worth Compass: Daily Practices for Revolutionary Living

Building unshakable worth isn't a one-time event. It is a daily practice of choosing sovereignty over diminishment, remembering over forgetting, embodiment over performance.

Morning Worth Attunement

Begin each day by placing both hands on your heart and declaring: *"I embody my divine worth today without apology or negotiation. I value my gifts appropriately. I serve from abundance, not depletion. Like Mary Magdalene with her alabaster jar, I know the sacred value of what I offer, and I share it with those ready to receive."*

This simple practice creates an energetic foundation that influences every interaction.

The Sacred Worth Check-In

Before discussing rates, creating offers, or setting boundaries, pause and ask:

- Am I honoring my worth in this decision, or am I shrinking to make others comfortable?
- Am I pricing from divine knowing or from fear of rejection?
- Does this boundary protect the sacred container of my work?

Adjust until your decision feels aligned with your deepest truth.

The Evidence Collection Practice

Keep a dedicated "Worth Witness" journal where you record:

- Specific transformations clients experience through your work
- Testimonials that reflect the profound value you create
- Moments where standing in your worth created positive ripples
- Instances where honoring your value led to better outcomes for everyone

Review this journal whenever worth doubts arise. Concrete proof is medicine for ancestral wounds.

The Evening Worth Integration

End each day by placing one hand on your heart and reflecting:

- How did I honor my worth today?
- Where did I maintain healthy worth boundaries?
- What moments can I celebrate where I valued my work appropriately?
- How can I deepen my worth embodiment tomorrow?

Sister, I want you to feel this truth in the very marrow of your bones:

You are the modern embodiment of Mary Magdalene's revolutionary worth. You carry an alabaster jar of precious medicine that this world desperately needs. When you honor the value of that medicine without apology or diminishment, when you break open that jar with sovereign certainty, you become a sacred wayshower for countless others still struggling to recognize their own immeasurable worth.

The worth revolution does not begin someday when you have more credentials or followers or external validation.

It begins TODAY. In this moment. With your very next decision about what you and your sacred work are truly worth.

Break open that alabaster jar, magnificent one. The world is ready for your fragrance to fill every room you enter.

A Love Letter from Mary Magdalene on Sacred Worth

Mary Magdalene appears in meditation, radiating the unshakeable certainty of someone who has never doubted her value.

My Beloved Daughter of Divine Worth,

Do you know what they never fully captured in the stories they tell about me? The unwavering certainty I felt as I carried my alabaster jar into that room. They speak of my devotion, yes, but rarely of my absolute knowing of both my worth and the value of my offering.

That jar contained a year's wages, they do record this fact. Yet what the stories fail to convey is that I never questioned whether my gift was worth the price. I never apologized for its extravagance. I never diminished its value to make others more comfortable with their own unworthiness.

When the criticism came, as it always does when a woman stands firmly in her worth, I did not defend or explain or justify. I simply stood in sovereign certainty of the value of both the gift and the giver.

This is the inheritance I offer you now, precious daughter.

Your worth is not something you must prove through achievements, earn through suffering, or justify through credentials. It is your divine birthright, recognized not created. When you price your sacred offerings, when you establish your boundaries, when you declare what you will and will not accept in exchange for your gifts, you are not being greedy or difficult or "too much."

You are being me. You are being the woman who knew without question that her most precious offering was worth a year's wages and offered it without hesitation, negotiation, or apology.

The world will try to convince you that your rates are too high, your boundaries too firm, your requirements too demanding. It will attempt to extract your medicine without proper exchange, to access your magic without appropriate investment, to receive your wisdom while questioning its value.

I tell you this with the authority of two thousand years: Stand unwavering in your worth, not from arrogance but from bone-deep knowing. Honor your medicine by valuing it properly. Create sacred containers through appropriate exchange. Your prosperity is not separate from your spirituality. It is the natural expression of divine value flowing through appropriate channels.

You do not need to defend your worth to anyone, ever. You need only to embody it so completely that others can feel its truth radiating from your very presence like sunlight from the sun.

Remember me not just as the devoted follower, but as the sovereign woman who knew her worth beyond all questioning. That is your inheritance. That is your birthright. That is your Magdalene legacy calling you home.

With eternal recognition of your immeasurable value,

—**Mary Magdalene**

"A woman who knows her worth changes not just her own life but the very economics of feminine wisdom in the world, for each time you stand firm in your value, you create a pathway for countless others to remember theirs."

—**Rose Wilder**

GATEWAY 2

Divine Timing—Success in Sacred Rhythm

"She who aligns with sacred timing dances with creation itself, neither rushing ahead nor lagging behind, but moving in perfect harmony with divine orchestration."

—*Rose Wilder*

While crafting these words about divine timing, I have been forced to surrender my own timeline multiple times for this book's completion. Life and the world conspired to slow me down through unexpected challenges, and I found myself either practicing what I teach about honoring natural rhythms or falling back into old patterns of pushing against the flow. Guess which approach created more ease and better writing?

The Divine Timing Revolution Your Soul Has Been Waiting For

Sister, can I share something that will LIBERATE your entire approach to success, purpose, and the divine unfolding of your work in the world?

Imagine yourself standing in the cool pre-dawn darkness outside a tomb. The air is thick with grief, uncertainty, and waiting. Everything you believed in seems to have died. Your hopes, your vision, your understanding of how things should unfold, all shattered.

And yet, something within you, some inexplicable KNOWING, has drawn you to this place before anyone else arrives.

This is Mary Magdalene at the tomb, arriving BEFORE dawn, before the stone was rolled away, before any visible evidence of resurrection appeared.

She did not arrive demanding immediate results. She did not attempt to force the stone to move through her own effort. She didn't pace anxiously, checking the position of the stars, wondering WHEN the miracle would happen.

She simply *showed up* and remained PRESENT to what was unfolding in divine timing. The resurrection wasn't rushed. The most profound miracle in spiritual history occurred in its PERFECT sacred moment, not a second too soon or too late.

And herein lies the most REVOLUTIONARY business principle I have discovered in my entire Magdalene journey:

Divine Timing always beats hustle. EVERY. SINGLE. TIME.

I can hear the bro marketing business gurus gasping in horror! "But what about deadlines? What about metrics? What about launch schedules? What about striking while the iron is hot, and killin' it, crushing it? What about beating the competition?"

These are the voices of a paradigm that believes we can somehow CONTROL time, FORCE outcomes, and OVERRIDE the natural rhythms of creation. And sister, I am here to tell you with every ounce of my being that this paradigm is not just exhausting, it's working in direct OPPOSITION to the way divine manifestation actually unfolds.

What if the timeline of your success has never been within your control? What if your current "delay" is actually divine PROTECTION? What if that launch that isn't coming together is actually making space for something far more ALIGNED? What if your body's call for rest isn't sabotage but sacred WISDOM?

Are you ready to step into the Magdalene way of divine timing? Because once you experience success in sacred rhythm rather than forced hustle, you will NEVER want to go back to the exhaustion of pushing against the natural flow of your life and business.

The Midnight Revelation That Changed Everything

Let me share a DEEPLY personal story that revolutionized my entire understanding of divine timing.

Years ago, I had fallen for the *have to's* and *shoulds* of traditional bro marketing, even though I had already achieved the abundance and harmony in my life and business that I desired. I found myself falling face-first into the trap of hustle culture and striving for numbers and things that I did not even truly align with or want.

I was sitting at my desk at 2:00 AM, tears streaming down my face, and a slight hiccup while I sobbed trying to finish the materials for my third launch that quarter. My body was absolutely screaming for rest. My creativity had dried up. My joy had vanished. Yet I kept pushing because that's what "successful" entrepreneurs do, right?

"Just one more email sequence," I told myself. "Just one more sales page. Just one more presentation script."

I was following all the "rules" of success, and yet something felt profoundly out of alignment. My body was in open rebellion. My mind couldn't focus. My soul felt like it was being crushed under the weight of artificial urgency.

That night, in a moment of complete surrender, I felt Mary Magdalene's presence so strongly it took my breath away. And I received this message with such clarity, it seemed to reverberate through my entire being:

"The cycles of death and rebirth cannot be rushed. The tomb time is sacred. The darkness before dawn is necessary."

In that moment, I understood something that transformed everything:

I was trying to skip the natural cycles of creation. I was attempting to move from seed to harvest without honoring the necessary darkness of germination, the slow unfurling of growth, the patient development of fruit.

I shut down my computer. I canceled the project. I took a complete business sabbatical for weeks.

The world would predict disaster: lost momentum, vanishing clients, diminished income. But what actually happened DEFIED all conventional business logic.

During that sacred pause:

- The exact direction my work needed to take became crystal clear
- A completely new restructuring downloaded that was far more aligned than what I had been forcing
- My energy and creativity returned in a POWERFUL surge, and I fell back in love with what I do
- And most surprisingly, my income INCREASED rather than decreased

Why? Because I finally aligned with divine timing rather than fighting against it. I surrendered to the wisdom of natural cycles rather than imposing artificial urgency. I honored the sacred rhythm of creation rather than the linear timeline of hustle culture.

This is the Magdalene way of divine timing, not the exhausting pursuit of forcing outcomes, yet the sovereign alignment with natural rhythms that allows your work to emerge in its perfect moment, just as the resurrection did not occur on Mary Magdalene's schedule but in the precise divine moment it was meant to unfold.

The Sacred Dance with Time

Mary Magdalene understood something that our modern world has forgotten: time is not linear, it's CYCLICAL. There are seasons for planting, seasons for growth, seasons for harvest, and seasons for lying fallow. When we honor these natural rhythms in our business, we align with the very forces of creation itself.

Consider these Magdalene truths about divine timing:

The pause is productive.

Mary Magdalene's vigil at the tomb wasn't passive waiting; it was ACTIVE PRESENCE, a sacred holding of space for the miracle to emerge. Your business "pauses" are not lost time. They are fertile ground for the next evolution.

My client was frustrated when her launch didn't materialize on schedule. Instead of pushing harder, we honored the pause. During this "inactive" period, she received the exact refinements her program needed to truly serve her audience. When the offering finally launched, three months later than planned, it filled within 72 hours.

Divine delay is often divine protection.

How many times have you looked back on something that didn't happen when you wanted it to, only to realize later you were being PROTECTED from something not truly aligned?

The contract that fell through that would have drained your energy for months. The client you didn't get who would have pulled you off purpose. The opportunity that vanished that would have taken you down a path misaligned with your soul's calling.

What we perceive as "delays" are often cosmic redirections guiding us toward our highest alignment.

Forcing timing creates upstream struggle.

When we push against the natural rhythm of our business cycles, we exhaust ourselves rowing upstream. When we surrender to divine timing, we find ourselves carried by currents of grace.

A client spent a year trying to force the launch of her offering, pushing against numerous technical difficulties, team misalignments, and her own health challenges. When she finally surrendered to divine timing and released her attachment to a specific launch date, everything fell into place with miraculous ease. The new products emerged three months later than her original "deadline" but with far greater power and reach.

Your body knows the timing your mind cannot calculate.

Mary Magdalene followed her body's knowing to the tomb before rational thought would have deemed it sensible. Your body's signals about timing transcend mental logic.

The exhaustion you feel isn't laziness, it's divine guidance about rhythm. The creative surge at "inconvenient" times isn't random, it's sacred timing. The resistance to moving forward isn't procrastination, it's your innate wisdom about divine unfolding.

Your body is the most sophisticated instrument for discerning divine timing in your business and life. When you override its signals in favor of artificial deadlines and arbitrary timelines, you disconnect from your most powerful source of guidance.

The Tomb Awakening Meditation: A Sacred Ceremony

Create sacred space with candles flickering and rose petals scattered.

This powerful meditation connects you with Mary Magdalene's wisdom of divine timing as she waited at the tomb, teaching you to trust the sacred unfolding of your business and life.

Sacred Intention: To deepen your trust in divine timing and develop patience with the sacred unfolding of your business cycles.

What You'll Need:

- A quiet, undisturbed space
- A candle

Divine Timing—Success in Sacred Rhythm

- A stone to represent the "tomb stone"
- A flower or seed to represent new emergence
- Optional: Soft music that evokes sacred waiting

The Ritual:

1. Creating Sacred Space

- Light your candle, saying: *"I illuminate the sacred space between what has ended and what is yet to be born."*
- Place your stone before, saying: *"This represents all that appears blocked or delayed in my life and business."*
- Place your flower/seed behind the stone, saying: *"This represents what is preparing to emerge in divine timing."*
- Sit comfortably, taking three deep breaths to center yourself.

2. The Vigil Meditation

- Close your eyes and visualize yourself sitting outside a tomb before dawn, just as Mary Magdalene did.
- Feel the cool night air, the darkness surrounding you, the stone firmly in place.
- Notice any feelings of impatience, anxiety, or doubt about what will unfold, or whether anything will happen at all.
- Breathe into these feelings, neither resisting nor attaching to them.
- Hear Mary Magdalene's voice whispering: *"The darkness before dawn is necessary. The waiting is part of the miracle."*
- Continue sitting in this sacred darkness, practicing being fully present without forcing anything to change.

3. The Divine Timing Activation

- As you sit in this space of sacred waiting, begin to sense subtle energies stirring behind the stone.
- Don't rush to move the stone; simply notice the preparations happening in divine timing.

- Feel Mary Magdalene's steady presence beside you, her unwavering trust in sacred unfolding.
- When you sense the moment is right (trust your intuition), gently move the stone aside.
- See your flower/seed illuminated in dawn's first light, perfectly timed in its emergence.
- Hear Mary Magdalene say: *"What unfolds in divine timing carries a power that forced manifestation can never achieve."*

4. *The Sacred Rhythms Integration*

    - Keeping your eyes closed, place one hand on your heart and one on your womb space.
    - Feel the natural rhythms of your own body... your heartbeat, your breath, your cyclical nature.
    - See how these same rhythms exist in your business... cycles of rest and activity, gestation and birth, death and rebirth.
    - Affirm: *"I surrender to divine timing in my business. I trust the sacred unfolding of my purpose. I honor both the waiting and the emergence as equally valuable."*

5. *Closing the Meditation*

    - Slowly open your eyes, remaining in the peaceful energy of divine timing.
    - Place both hands on your stone, feeling any remaining resistance to divine timing.
    - Move the stone completely aside, fully revealing your flower/seed.
    - Say: *"I align with sacred timing in all aspects of my business. I trust the perfect unfolding of divine orchestration. And so it is."*
    - Blow out your candle, carrying this trust in divine timing into your day.

Practice this meditation whenever you feel impatient with timing, anxious about delays, or tempted to force things to happen faster than their natural rhythm.

Divine Timing as Your Daily Compass

While the big seasonal shifts are important, divine timing is ultimately cultivated through daily awareness and micro-adjustments. Here are POWERFUL practices to integrate into your business rhythm:

Morning Energy Reading

Before planning your day's activities, tune into your energetic state:

- Place one hand on your heart and one on your womb space
- Take three deep breaths, allowing yourself to feel your true energy level and quality
- Ask: *"What is my natural energy supporting today? What flow am I in?"*
- Adjust your daily plan to align with this energy rather than forcing a predetermined schedule

I transform productivity with this simple practice. Instead of pushing through my to-do list in order, I now ask which tasks align and flow with my current energy. Some days that means creative work, other days administrative tasks, maybe a blend throughout the day, and sometimes rest. By following my energy rather than fighting it, I accomplish more with less struggle. Always honor your energetic blueprint and design in this way. As part of your Alabaster Jar Bundle, you will receive a copy of your energetic blueprint.

The Sacred Pause

Throughout your day, practice conscious pausing when you feel resistance:

- Place your hands on your heart
- Ask: *"Is this resistance a sign that timing isn't aligned? Or is it simply procrastination?"*
- Listen for the subtle difference between divine guidance and fear-based avoidance
- Follow what your body wisdom reveals

The Three Divine Timing Questions

When making any significant business decision, ask these three questions:

1. Is this the natural season for this action in my business cycle?
2. Does this feel like swimming upstream or flowing with the current?
3. Am I moving from divine guidance or from fear of missing out?

These questions create a powerful discernment filter for aligning with divine timing.

The Evening Integration

End each business day with a brief timing practice:

- Acknowledge what phase of your larger business cycle you are currently in
- Celebrate moments when you honored divine timing today
- Release any attempts to force outcomes against their natural unfolding
- Set intention to deepen your trust in sacred timing tomorrow

The most revolutionary aspect of divine timing is this: When you stop exhausting yourself by pushing against natural rhythms, you discover that success unfolds with greater ease, power, and sustainability than you ever imagined possible through constant striving.

A client of mine discovered this when she finally stopped forcing herself to write to completion against her intense resistance. She took a three-month sabbatical from writing, during which a completely new structure landed for her that transformed her entire approach. When she returned to writing, the book flowed with miraculous ease and was completed in half the time she had originally allocated, with far greater depth and impact.

This is the paradox of divine timing: What appears to be "delay" often creates acceleration. What feels like "waiting" is actually active preparation. What seems like "lost time" becomes your greatest efficiency.

Divine Timing—Success in Sacred Rhythm

From Linear Goals to Spiral Emergence

The Magdalene way of divine timing invites a complete reimagining of how we approach goals and visions for our business. Instead of the conventional linear path, with its rigid timelines, fixed outcomes, and straight-line thinking, we enter the sacred spiral of emergence.

Traces a spiral in the air with fluid movement.

In the spiral model of divine timing:

- Success unfolds through cycles rather than straight lines
- Vision emerges and refines rather than remaining static
- Outcomes often exceed our limited imagination when we surrender to divine orchestration
- Each apparent "ending" becomes the seed for the next beginning

A client who experienced this transformation when her carefully planned program launch "failed" to materialize on schedule. Instead of forcing it or abandoning it, she surrendered to divine timing. What emerged six months later wasn't just a better version of her original vision, it was an entirely new model of client transformation that far exceeded what she had initially imagined.

"If my original timeline had manifested," she told me in wonder, "I would have created something good but limited. By surrendering to divine timing, I received something miraculous that would never have occurred to my strategic mind to create."

This is the ultimate liberation of divine timing. When you release your attachment to how and when your vision must materialize, you open to possibilities far beyond what your limited human perspective can conceive. You become a co-creator with divine intelligence rather than a lone striver trying to force outcomes through sheer will.

Mary Magdalene demonstrated this surrender at the tomb. She did not arrive with a fixed vision of how resurrection would look or when it would happen. She simply showed up in faith, remained present to the unfolding, and witnessed a miracle beyond human comprehension.

Your business, your creative work, your divine calling, all are seeds of resurrection in their own right, meant to emerge not on your demanding timeline but in perfect divine orchestration. When you trust this timing, when you align with these natural rhythms, you enter a flow of manifestation that feels like magic compared to the exhaustion of constant pushing.

This is the Magdalene way of divine timing, success in sacred rhythm, dancing with creation itself, neither rushing ahead nor lagging behind, but moving in perfect harmony with the divine orchestration of your purpose.

A Love Letter from Mary Magdalene on Divine Timing

Mary Magdalene sits in profound stillness at the threshold between night and dawn, embodying the exquisite patience of one who has witnessed the perfect unfolding of divine miracles.

My Beloved Daughter of Sacred Timing,

Do you know why I came to the tomb before dawn? Not because I was impatient for resurrection to begin, but because my heart was so attuned to the sacred rhythms of creation that I felt the exact moment when death would transform into life. I arrived not to force the stone to roll away, but to witness the perfect unfolding of divine timing.

The world tells you that success requires constant pushing, relentless forward motion, and the brutal override of natural cycles. It sells you the lie that if you're not growing every quarter, expanding every month, launching every season, you are somehow failing or falling behind.

Yet I, apostle to the apostles, tell you this: The most profound transformations happen not through force but through perfect surrender to divine timing. The stone was not moved by human hands straining against its weight. It rolled away at the precise moment ordained by infinite wisdom.

Your business is also governed by these same sacred laws. There are seasons for planting and seasons for harvest, times for outward expression and times for inward reflection, moments for bold action and moments for patient waiting. When you align with these natural rhythms rather than fighting against them, you become a co-creator with the very forces that orchestrate miracles.

I have watched from beyond time as countless spiritual entrepreneurs exhaust themselves swimming upstream against their own divine flow. I have seen brilliant women burn out trying to maintain linear growth in a cyclical universe. I have witnessed sacred missions collapse under the weight of artificial urgency when they could have flourished through patient trust in perfect timing.

The tomb time is sacred, beloved. The darkness before dawn is necessary. The pause between death and rebirth cannot be rushed. When your business feels stuck, when your vision seems delayed, when nothing appears to be happening, this is not failure. This is gestation. This is the deep work happening beneath the surface that makes true emergence possible.

Just as the seed must rest in dark soil before it can reach toward light, your dreams require periods of invisible development. Just as the moon must wane before it can wax full again, your success must breathe in cycles of expansion and contraction. Just as winter must fully arrive before spring can authentically begin, your business must honor necessary endings before new beginnings can take root.

This is not passive waiting but active trust. This is not lazy inaction but conscious alignment. This is not spiritual bypassing but divine intelligence in motion.

When you stop forcing and start flowing, when you release artificial timelines and embrace sacred timing, when you trust the perfect unfolding rather than demanding immediate results, you align with the same power that moved mountains, parted seas, and rolled away stones thought too heavy for human hands.

Your most profound breakthroughs will not come through pushing harder but through surrendering deeper. Your greatest successes will not emerge from following artificial deadlines but from honoring the organic timing of your soul's evolution. Your most sustainable growth will not happen through constant acceleration but through the sacred dance of expansion and integration.

Remember me not as the woman who waited by the tomb, but as the woman who trusted so completely in divine timing that I was positioned to witness the impossible become inevitable. That same trust I offer you now: the knowing that what is meant for you will not pass you by, that delays are often protection, that your breakthrough is being perfectly orchestrated even when you cannot see the evidence.

Trust the timing of your life, beloved. Trust the rhythm of your business. Trust the perfect unfolding of your sacred purpose. For in this trust, you align with the very heartbeat of creation itself.

The world will try to convince you that divine timing is a luxury you cannot afford, that waiting is weakness, that patience is procrastination. But I tell you this truth that echoes through eternity: Nothing truly magnificent has ever been rushed. Every masterpiece requires its perfect season. Every miracle unfolds in its divinely appointed moment.

Your business is not behind schedule, precious sister. Your dreams are not delayed. Your purpose is not forgotten. You are exactly where you need to be in this moment, learning exactly what you need to learn, developing exactly the strength and wisdom you'll need for what's coming.

The stone will roll away when it's time. The tomb will reveal its treasure when the moment is right. Your breakthrough will come not when you demand it but when you're perfectly prepared to receive it.

Until then, practice the sacred art of divine waiting. Not anxious waiting that depletes your energy, but expectant waiting that builds your faith. Not passive waiting that abandons action, but aligned waiting that takes inspired steps when the inner green light appears.

This is how you honor both the timing and the miracle, by trusting the process completely while remaining ready to move when the divine moment arrives.

I am with you in the sacred space between what has ended and what is yet to be born. I am with you in the holy pause before your greatest emergence. I am with you as you learn to dance with divine timing rather than wrestle against it.

Your time is coming, beloved. Trust the sacred unfolding.

With eternal love and perfect trust in your divine timing,

—**Mary Magdalene**

"She who aligns with sacred timing accomplishes more through divine flow than others achieve through endless striving, for she works with the forces of creation rather than against them, dancing with eternity rather than racing against time."

—***Rose Wilder***

GATEWAY 3

Authentic Power—Truth as Your Business Force

Confession: While writing this section on speaking truth without apology, I caught myself watering down my message in three different client communications. Each time, I had to pause, remember Mary Magdalene's unwavering certainty, and rewrite from my authentic voice. The practice is not about getting it right every time. It is about catching ourselves and returning to truth.

The Revolutionary Power of Undiluted Truth

When a woman speaks her truth, even if her entire body and her voice shakes, she transforms not only herself but the very world that tried to silence her.

Have you ever felt it? That electrifying moment when your truth rises up like a sacred flame, burning so bright within you that your skin can barely contain it? That instant when your inner knowing speaks with such unwavering clarity that all the external noise, the "shoulds" and "supposed-tos" and "best practices," suddenly falls away like autumn leaves?

Sister, THAT is the first whisper of your authentic power awakening.

When Mary Magdalene ran from the empty tomb to tell the disciples about the resurrection, she didn't craft a carefully worded message designed to appeal to their skepticism. She did not conduct market research to determine the most effective way to communicate her experience. She did not dilute her truth to make it more believable.

She simply spoke what she had witnessed with quiet, unwavering certainty.

"I have seen the Lord," she said. (John 20:18)

Five simple words that changed all of history.

Let that sink in for a moment, gorgeous. No elaborate marketing. No carefully crafted messaging strategy. No focus group testing to see how her truth would be received. Just the raw undiluted power of a woman who trusted her own experience so completely that she was willing to stake everything in it... her reputation, her credibility, her standing in the community... all for the sake of speaking what she knew to be true.

And when they doubted her, as the world often doubts women who speak uncomfortable truths, she did not backpedal or apologize or question her own experience. She stood firmly in her knowing, rooted in the power of her undiluted truth.

This, beloved, is authentic power.

Not power over others. Not power through manipulation or force. But power from within, the kind that cannot be granted by external authorities because it flows from the unwavering certainty of your own lived experience.

The Divine Compass Within You

Every woman alive today carries within her the same divine compass that guided Mary Magdalene, that fierce, unapologetic knowing that transcends logic and speaks directly from soul to soul. This is not some mystical gift bestowed only upon the chosen; it is your birthright as a woman, encoded in your very cells.

In a world drowning in strategies and formulas, your inner guidance system is the beacon that will never lead you astray. It speaks to you through:

- The full-body YES that ripples through you when something aligns with your truth
- The subtle contraction in your solar plexus when something isn't quite right
- The dream that returns night after night, carrying wisdom your conscious mind hasn't yet grasped
- The synchronicities that appear precisely when you are aligned with your authentic path
- The knowing that arrives without justification or evidence, yet carries absolute certainty

Your discernment is not just a quaint "women's intuition" to be acknowledged then ignored in favor of "more practical" approaches. It is the most sophisticated GPS system for navigating business and life, one that integrates information from your body, emotions, mind, and spirit to guide you toward your highest expression.

The Courage to Stand Alone in Your Knowing

Let's be REAL about what it takes to trust your inner guidance in a world that has spent centuries telling women to doubt themselves. It takes magnificent courage to stand firm when:

- Industry "experts" insist there's only one way to succeed
- Peers raise eyebrows at your unconventional approach
- Family members worry you're taking too many risks
- Your own inner critic whispers that you must be wrong

Mary Magdalene knew what it meant to stand alone in her truth. When she proclaimed the resurrection, she didn't have consensus or external validation. She had only her direct experience and the audacity to honor it above all else.

One of my clients, a brilliant healer with profound intuitive abilities, had spent years contorting herself to fit business models that contradicted everything her inner guidance told her. Her authentic knowing whispered that her work required deep, unhurried connection, yet she kept creating "scalable" programs because that's what the experts recommended.

"I don't think I'm cut out for business," she confessed, tears streaming down her face.

The truth was simpler and far more revolutionary: she wasn't cut out for someone else's business. She was being called to create a model as unique as her gifts.

Together, we dismantled the borrowed structures and external expectations. We excavated her authentic truth about healing, service, and value exchange. From that foundation of authenticity, we built a business model that followed her inner guidance rather than external formulas.

Six months later? Her practice began BLOOMING with aligned clients. Her work had deepened exponentially. Her energy had returned with such force that she felt like she could light up a city.

"The difference," she told me, "is that I'm no longer trying to convince anyone of anything. I'm simply sharing what I know to be true and allowing it to resonate with those who are meant to receive it."

THAT, beloved, is the Magdalene way, to speak your truth not as persuasion but as offering, trusting that those who are meant to receive it will recognize its value without endless convincing.

Activating Your Truth Transmission

Your authentic power is not just a personal resource, it is a revolutionary force that changes how you show up in your business and the world. When you speak from this place of bone-deep knowing:

- Your words carry an energetic resonance that transcends their literal meaning
- Your presence becomes magnetic without effort or strategy
- Your offerings attract precisely the people they're meant to serve
- Your impact expands exponentially beyond what forced marketing

could achieve

I call this "energetic integrity," the perfect alignment between what you know to be true, what you say, and how you say it. When these three elements harmonize, you activate a force field of authentic power that draws your aligned clients to you like moths to a magnificent flame.

I discovered this when I stopped crafting my message to please everyone, filtering what I would say, and how I would say it, and started speaking from my unfiltered truth about feminine leadership. My first authentic video, recorded in one take, without scripts or strategizing, reached many times my usual audience and brought dream clients seemingly out of nowhere.

I didn't do anything different marketing-wise, I just stopped worrying about how I would be received and spoke directly from my knowing.

That is the thing about truth transmission, it does not require elaborate strategies. Often, the simplest, most direct expression carries the strongest resonance.

Breaking the Chains of External Validation

Let's talk about the most radical aspect of authentic power: non-attachment to reception.

This is where most women get stuck. We speak our truth but then immediately scan the horizon for validation, approval, and agreement. We share our knowing but then measure its value by likes, comments, shares, and sales.

Mary Magdalene gives us a different model. When the disciples didn't believe her resurrection story, she didn't launch into desperate attempts to convince them. She didn't modify her message to make it more palatable. She simply stood in her knowing, allowing it to be received by those ready to hear it.

This non-attachment to external validation is the secret sauce of authentic power. It frees you from the exhausting cycle of seeking approval and allows your truth to stand sovereign, regardless of how it's received.

This is CHALLENGING, I get it. It goes against everything we've been taught about validation seeking. But it is also gloriously liberating.

When you release the need for everyone to "get it," you create space for those who are genuinely meant to receive your medicine to recognize it without all your energetic gymnastics trying to persuade them.

The Path from Strategic Content to Truth Transmission

Bounces with excitement because this changes EVERYTHING.

The journey from calculated messaging to authentic power requires a fundamental shift in how you approach the content you share in your business. This isn't about abandoning all strategy but rather ensuring that strategy serves your truth rather than diluting it.

Consider these transformative shifts:

From Market Research to Soul Inquiry

Instead of: "What's performing well in my industry?"

Ask: "What truth is living in me that seeks expression? What have I witnessed that others need to hear?"

From Formula to Authentic Voice

Instead of: Following the problem-agitate-solve approach

Allow: Your natural voice and rhythm to emerge, whether you speak in stories, questions, or direct declarations

From Strategic Vulnerability to Genuine Disclosure

Instead of: Calculating which personal struggles will create connection

Share: Only what genuinely serves your audience from a place of wholeness, not as manipulation

From Persuasion to Offering

Instead of: Creating content designed to convince

Simply: Offer your truth as a gift that those who need it can receive

An energy healer client made this shift with extraordinary results. After years of crafting "convincing" content about energy healing's validity, she began simply sharing from direct experience, specific transformations she'd witnessed, and unique understandings from her practice.

"I was TERRIFIED," she told me, laughing. "I kept thinking, 'This is too simple. No one will be convinced by this.' But what happened was exactly the opposite. Instead of having to convince people, I found myself connecting with those who already recognized the truth in what I was sharing. The quality of my clients completely transformed."

This is the power of truth transmission, not endless convincing but sovereign offering that naturally attracts those meant to receive it.

Ceremony: Standing in Your Truth Like Magdalene

This powerful ritual activates your authentic power and strengthens your ability to stand firmly in your truth, even when it contradicts conventional wisdom or faces doubt from others.

Sacred Intention: To embody the unwavering certainty of Mary Magdalene as she proclaimed her truth, activating your authentic power as the foundation of your business.

What You'll Need:

- A candle
- A small mirror
- A clear quartz crystal or stone (representing clarity of truth)
- Paper and pen
- A bell or chime (optional)

The Ceremony

1. *Creating Sacred Space*

   - Light your candle, saying: *"I illuminate the path of authentic power."*
   - Place your crystal between you and the candle, saying: *"I activate clarity of truth in all my expressions."*
   - Take three deep breaths, centering yourself in sacred presence.

2. *Claiming Your Authentic Message*

   - On your paper, write: "The truth I know that I've been afraid to fully express is…"
   - Allow yourself to write freely, without editing or censoring.
   - When complete, hold the paper to your heart and say: *"This is my knowing. This is my medicine. This is my truth."*

3. *The Mary Magdalene Embodiment*

   - Pick up your crystal and hold it at your throat center (communication center).
   - Close your eyes and visualize Mary Magdalene on Easter morning, having just witnessed the empty tomb and the risen Christ.
   - Feel her certainty, her clarity, her unwavering knowing despite the doubt she would face.
   - Allow her energy to merge with yours, feeling her authentic power flowing into your being.
   - When this merge feels complete, say aloud: *"I embody the authentic power of Mary Magdalene, who stood firmly in her truth even when alone in her knowing."*

4. *The Truth Declaration*

   - Hold your mirror in one hand and your crystal in the other.
   - Look into your own eyes in the mirror.
   - Speaking directly to your reflection, declare your truth aloud, beginning with *"I know…"* or *"I have seen…"*

- Speak slowly, with sovereign certainty, allowing each word to carry the full weight of your authentic power.
- Do not justify, explain, or qualify your knowing. Simply state it with the quiet certainty of one who knows what they know.

5. *The Power Activation*

    - After speaking your truth, continue gazing into your own eyes.
    - Place your crystal on your heart.
    - Say: *"I stand in my truth not to convince or persuade, but because it is who I am. My authentic power flows not from external validation but from internal certainty. I honor my knowing as my greatest business asset."*
    - Ring your bell or chime, allowing its vibration to seal this activation.

6. *The Sacred Integration*

    - Pick up your paper with your written truth.
    - Read it once more, feeling the difference in how it resonates now compared to when you first wrote it.
    - Consider how this truth will inform your business moving forward, not as a strategy but as a foundation.
    - Place the paper under your crystal beside your candle, saying: *"My truth is clear. My power is activated. My message is sovereign."*

7. *Closing the Ceremony*

    - Place one hand on your heart and one on your throat.
    - Take three deep breaths, feeling your authentic power fully integrated.
    - Say: *"Like Mary Magdalene, I stand in my truth with quiet certainty. I speak from direct experience. I trust my knowing above all external voices. And so it is."*
    - Extinguish your candle or allow it to burn completely (safely).

Keep your crystal with you during business conversations or content creation as a reminder of your commitment to authentic power. Return to this ritual whenever you feel yourself doubting your truth or tempted to dilute your message.

Calibrating Your Inner Guidance System

*Excitement because this is the practical magic, dear Maverick.

Your inner guidance system is like any powerful instrument, it becomes more precise with regular use and attunement. Here are practical ways to sharpen your discernment and strengthen your connection to your authentic knowing:

The Body Truth Check

Your body never lies. Before making any business decision, pause and scan your physical sensations:

- Where do you feel expansion or contraction?
- Does your breath deepen or become shallow?
- Does your energy rise or fall?
- What specific sensations arise in your gut, heart, or throat?

These physical responses are your truth-meter, often registering alignment or misalignment before your conscious mind can process it.

The Sacred Pause Practice

In our rush to respond, decide, and act, we often override our inner knowing. Commit to taking a sacred pause before any significant business decision:

- Take three conscious breaths
- Place a hand on your heart center
- Ask: "What do I know about this beyond what I think about this?"
- Allow your response to arise without forcing or analyzing

Even 30 seconds of sacred pause can radically alter your business trajectory by creating space for your authentic knowing to emerge.

The Discernment Journal

Start tracking the relationship between your intuitive hits and their outcomes:

- Record your initial gut feelings about business decisions
- Note when you follow your inner guidance versus external advice
- Document the results that follow
- Look for patterns in your accuracy

Over time, this creates undeniable evidence of your inner guidance system's reliability, building your trust in it.

The Inner Mentor Dialogue

Establish a regular practice of consulting your internal wisdom as you would a trusted mentor:

- Create a sacred space free from distractions
- Bring specific business questions to this space
- Write or speak these questions clearly
- Allow responses to flow without editing or censoring
- Express gratitude for the wisdom received

Think of this not as talking to yourself but as accessing the deepest wellspring of knowing within you, the same source that guided Mary Magdalene to the tomb when others remained hidden in fear.

Daily Practice: Speaking Your Truth with Quiet Confidence

Integrate these practices into your daily business rhythm to strengthen your authentic power:

Morning Truth Activation

Before engaging with any external input (technology, media, email, news), sit in silence with your hand on your heart and ask:

"What truth is longing to be expressed through me today?"

Listen for the whisper of your authentic voice. Write down what you receive without editing.

Commit to sharing this truth in some form during your day, whether through content, in client conversations, or in how you structure your business activities.

The Magdalene Pause

When faced with business decisions or content creation, practice what I call "The Magdalene Pause"—a moment of inner listening before external expression.

Pause, breathe deeply, and ask:

- Is this truly my voice or am I echoing someone else's formula?
- Does this expression feel aligned with my soul's knowing?
- Am I speaking/creating/deciding from authentic power or from fear?

Adjust as needed until you feel the resonance of your authentic truth.

Truth Before Tactics

Before implementing any business strategy or marketing tactic, filter it through your authentic knowing:

1. Does this approach honor my values and lived experience?
2. Can I adapt this to express my authentic voice rather than following a formula?
3. If this doesn't resonate, what alternative would better express my truth?

Remember: Effective business strategies flow from authentic expression, not the other way around.

The Daily Non-Apology

Pay attention to how often you apologize for or diminish your truth in business contexts:

- "This might sound strange, yet..."
- "I'm not sure if this is right, yet..."
- "This is just my opinion, yet..."

Each time you catch yourself diminishing your truth, restate your expression without the apology or qualifier. Practice owning your knowing with the quiet confidence of Mary Magdalene.

A Message from Mary Magdalene on Authentic Power

Beloved Holy Truth-Bearer,

Do you know why they called me "apostle to the apostles"? Not because I was louder or more persuasive or more strategic in my communication. They called me this because when all others fled or hid or doubted, I stood firmly in what I had witnessed.

"I have seen the Lord." (John 20:28)

Those five simple words. No elaborate explanations. No desperate attempts to convince. Just the quiet, unwavering certainty of a woman who trusts her own experience above all external doubts.

This is the authentic power I offer you now, not power that requires credentials or followers or algorithms or approval. This is the power that flows from within, from the unwavering trust in what you have lived, what you have witnessed, what you know in the marrow of your bones to be true.

The world will try to complicate this. It will tell you that your voice needs strategies and formulas and frameworks to be heard. It will suggest that your truth needs enhancement, polishing, and packaging to be received.

I tell you this: The most powerful message is the most authentic one. The most magnetic force is unwavering truth. The most effective business strategy is the one that honors your lived experience above all external pressures.

Stand in this knowing, beloved. Speak your truth not to convince but to offer. Trust that those who are meant to receive your medicine will recognize its value without endless persuasion.

Your authentic voice is not just your power, it is your divine birthright and your sacred offering to a world drowning in strategic communication but thirsting for undiluted truth.

With eternal recognition of your authentic power,

—**Mary Magdalene**

"When a woman honors her lived experience as her greatest wisdom, she steps into an authentic power that no external authority can grant or remove, for true power is not conferred from without but recognized from within."

—*Rose Wilder*

GATEWAY 4

Sacred Circle—Creating Your Soul Business Community

"True influence is not measured by how many you reach, but by how deeply you connect."
—*Rose Wilder*

Tonight it is now just after 2 AM, and I am once again rewriting this chapter for the third time because life just handed me another opportunity to practice what I teach. Tonight's lesson: Sometimes the most profound purpose-led business principles is knowing when to rest instead of push. Even this book had to be written the Magdalene way, in divine timing, not my preferred timeline.

The Forgotten Legacy of Mary Magdalene's Circle

Have you ever felt the aching loneliness of building a business in isolation? That peculiar modern paradox of being "connected" to thousands online yet feeling utterly alone in your work? That exhausting hamster wheel of "networking" that feels way more like speed-dating than soul connection?

Sweet sister, I have REVOLUTIONARY news that's going to flip your entire approach to business community upside down and inside out!

The Mary Magdalene you have never been told about? She was not a solitary follower. She was a MASTERFUL community builder who understood something about connection that most of today's "networking experts" have completely missed.

When we dive into the stories of Mary Magdalene beyond the limited mainstream narrative, we discover a woman who gathered and held the early movement together after the crucifixion when fear had scattered the disciples. The Gospel of Mary reveals she didn't do this through clever marketing or strategic alliances. She did it through DEEP, AUTHENTIC CONNECTION with those who resonated with her message.

And here's the STUNNING difference between her approach and what we are taught today:

Modern business tells us to build the BIGGEST audience possible, to reach thousands or millions through clever marketing, to prioritize scale over depth.

Mary Magdalene understood that true transformation happens in SACRED CIRCLE, in the intimate container of a soul-aligned community where authentic connection creates the space for absolute MAGIC.

This isn't merely spiritual teaching. This is PRACTICAL BUSINESS WISDOM for sensitive maverick entrepreneurs who know in their bones there must be a better way than the endless exhaustion of trying to appeal to everyone.

The Upper Room: Mary Magdalene's First Sacred Circle

Let's time-travel together to one of the most overlooked moments of Mary Magdalene's leadership, the gathering in the upper room after the crucifixion.

Imagine the scene: The movement seems on the verge of collapse. The followers are scattered in fear. Everything they have built together appears to be crumbling.

Yet historical and apocryphal accounts tell us that Mary Magdalene gathered the followers in the upper room, creating a sacred container for grief, confusion, and ultimately, revelation.

She understood a fundamental truth: You have to GET IN THE ROOM where transformation happens.

This wasn't just any room. This "upper room" became the first sacred circle of the early movement, a space where authentic connection transcended hierarchy, where deep truth could be spoken without fear, where transformation was held in the container of community rather than isolated individualism.

Do you see the REVOLUTIONARY implications for your business?

True movements don't spread through mass marketing to strangers. They spread through the RIPPLE EFFECT of deeply transformed individuals who cannot help but share what they've experienced.

But first, you have to GET IN THE ROOM.

This is the profound difference between networking and sacred circle:

Networking seeks to maximize connections, often prioritizing quantity over quality, strategic advantage over authentic alignment.

It asks: "How can this person help me achieve my goals?" You show up to GET FROM the room.

Sacred Circle cultivates soul-level relationships with those who share your values and vision.

It asks: "How can we journey together in service to something greater than ourselves?" You show up to GET IN the room—fully present, fully committed, fully aligned.

The first approach leaves you DEPLETED. The second approach leaves you ENERGIZED.

The first approach feels like WORK. The second approach feels like COMING HOME.

Mary Magdalene knew: The magic happens when you GET IN THE ROOM where souls gather in sacred purpose.

From Exhaustion to Exhilaration in Your Business Community

Let me share something deeply personal, something I rarely talk about but that changed EVERYTHING for me.

For a time, I gave in to the pressure and followed the conventional wisdom about building a business community. I measured success by traditional marketing standards, followers, subscribers, and engagement metrics. I exhausted myself trying to be visible to EVERYONE, to network in all the right places, to cast the widest possible net.

The result? A large yet lukewarm, unengaged list. Numbers, yet not a thriving community. Endless energy drain and a persistent feeling that despite "knowing" thousands, I was somehow still profoundly alone in my business.

Then came my breakdown, or rather, my beautiful BREAKTHROUGH.

After a particularly exhausting business expansion that left me physically ill from overextension, I retreated into silence. And in that silence, I heard Mary Magdalene's wisdom with stunning clarity:

"Stop trying to reach everyone. Start connecting deeply with the few who are truly yours to serve."

With trembling hands yet a resolute heart, I made the most TERRIFYING business decision of my life:

I let go of 90% of my "community." I completely unplugged from social media and hustle. I canceled events and engagements aimed at growing my audience.

Instead, I focused once again on what had always proved to be my superpower, nurturing DEEP, MEANINGFUL connections with my existing sacred circle, those clients and colleagues whose souls seemed to recognize mine on a level beyond strategic business alignment.

What happened next DEFIED all conventional business logic.

My income did not plummet, it DOUBLED. My impact did not diminish, it DEEPENED. My energy did not deplete, it EXPANDED. And still continues to many years later.

And most surprisingly, my businesses did not become smaller. They GREW yet in an organic way guided by resonance rather than reach.

This is the Magdalene way of sacred circle: not the exhausting pursuit of ever-larger audiences, but the sovereign cultivation of soul-deep connection with those who are truly yours to serve.

The Magdalene Principles of Sacred Circle

Mary Magdalene's approach to community reveals several KEY principles that can transform how you build your business relationships:

Soul Recognition Over Strategic Connection

Mary Magdalene did not choose her circle based on who could advance her cause most effectively. She gathered those whose souls recognized the truth she carried.

In your business, this means prioritizing authentic resonance over strategic advantage when building relationships. It means asking not "Who would be helpful to know?" but "With whom do I feel that inexplicable soul recognition?"

I transformed my entire approach to business relationships with this simple shift. Instead of forcing connections with "influencers" in my field, I began cultivating relationships that felt naturally aligned. Within months, I had created a close-knit community of colleagues who became not just business associates but genuine soul friends who supported each other's work in organic, powerful ways.

Depth Over Breadth

The Gospel of Mary shows her sharing her deepest teachings with those ready to receive them, rather than diluting her message to reach a wider audience.

In your business, this means creating experiences of profound depth for the few rather than surface engagement with the many. It means being willing to go DEEP even if it means reaching fewer people initially.

When I replaced a weekly newsletter going out with a quarterly in-depth custom email sent to a much smaller list of genuinely engaged readers, the response was IMMEDIATE and POWERFUL. "I've never had so many meaningful responses," my assistant shared with me in amazement during our next meeting. "People are actually engaging with the content in a way they never have before!"

Authentic Truth Over Acceptable Messaging

Even when the male disciples challenged her, Mary Magdalene spoke her truth without dilution.

In your business, this means attracting your community through authentic expression rather than strategically crafted messaging designed to appeal to the masses. It means having the courage to say what others might not, knowing that your truth will resonate deeply with those meant to hear it.

A client had been carefully crafting her message to avoid controversy. When she finally spoke her unfiltered truth about her faith and feminine spirituality, she was terrified of alienating people. Instead, her authentic voice magnetized exactly the community that she had been trying to reach all along.

Mutual Empowerment Over Hierarchical Leadership

Mary Magdalene did not position herself above her community but among them, recognizing the divine wisdom in each person.

In your business, this means creating collaborative relationships rather than positioning yourself as the sole expert or authority. It means recognizing and honoring the wisdom, gifts, and contributions of your community members.

Sustained Connection Over Transactional Engagement

The early community gathered regularly for deep sharing, not just when there was something to be gained.

In your business, this means nurturing an ongoing relationship rather than engaging only when you have something to promote or need something in return. It means creating spaces for connection that aren't driven by an immediate business outcome.

When you build your business community based on these Magdalene principles, something MIRACULOUS happens: You create a sacred container for transformation that benefits not just your clients but yourself. You develop relationships that ENERGIZE rather than deplete. You cultivate a community that becomes not just the recipients of your work but co-creators of your evolving mission.

This is the sacred physics of soul-aligned community: The energy generated through authentic connection creates a field of possibility far more powerful than anything you could create alone.

From Mass Marketing to Soul Magnetism

The shift from conventional audience-building to sacred circle creation requires a fundamental reorientation in how you approach community in your business. This isn't about abandoning all efforts to share your work but rather transforming the energy behind those efforts.

Consider these paradigm-shifting approaches:

From Targeting to Invitation

Instead of: Strategically targeting specific demographics or psychographics

Focus on: Extending soulful invitations to those who resonate with your truth

Mary Magdalene did not target the disciples; she created a space of authentic welcome for those drawn to her circle. There's a WORLD of difference between targeting someone as a potential client and inviting them into sacred space as a welcomed participant.

I had a client who stopped "targeting ideal clients" and started "extending heartfelt invitations to kindred spirits." She was amazed at how differently people responded to her. "It doesn't even feel like marketing anymore," she told me. "It feels like hosting a beautiful gathering where exactly the right people show up."

From Automation to Attunement

Instead of: Creating automated sequences to "nurture" connections

Focus on: Energetic attunement to what your community truly needs in each moment

While systems and structures have their place, sacred circle thrives on energetic attunement rather than automated sequences. This means being genuinely present with your community, feeling into what's needed rather than following predetermined paths.

From Performance to Presence

Instead of: Constantly performing for your audience

Focus on: Cultivating authentic presence that allows your community to experience the real you

Release the exhaustion of constant performance for your audience. Instead, cultivate authentic presence that allows your community to experience the real you rather than a carefully curated version designed to impress or engage.

From Numbers to Connection

Instead of: Focusing on growing your numbers

Focus on: Deepening your connections

Shift your focus from growing your numbers to deepening your connections. One soul-aligned relationship that flourishes through genuine recognition creates more business magic than hundreds of lukewarm followers.

From Conversion to Co-Creation

Instead of: Seeing your community as people to convert into clients

Focus on: Recognizing them as co-creators in an evolving sacred mission

Perhaps most revolutionary, stop seeing your community as people to convert into clients. Instead, recognize them as co-creators in an evolving sacred mission that benefits from their particular gifts and perspectives.

I witnessed this shift transform the business of a gifted intuitive who came to me burned out from her efforts to build a large online community.

"I'm doing everything right according to the marketing experts," she told me, "creating daily content, running engagement campaigns, optimizing my funnel, but I feel completely disconnected from the people I'm supposedly serving."

Together, we dismantled her marketing strategy and replaced it with a sacred circle approach. Instead of creating content for a faceless audience, she began writing letters to her "soul-aligned few." Instead of focusing on growing her email list, she created meaningful rituals for her existing community. Instead of constant promotional sequences, she developed genuine relationships through authentic sharing.

"The most surprising shift," she told me six months later, "is that I no longer feel alone in my business. These aren't just 'followers' anymore; they are my sacred circle, people who truly see me and whom I truly see in return. And somehow, even though my list is smaller, my income has doubled because the connections are so much more aligned."

This is the MAGIC of sacred circle in business, not the exhausting pursuit of audience growth but the sovereign cultivation of soul-aligned community that generates abundance through resonance rather than reach.

Ceremony: Soul Client Connection Meditation

This powerful meditation helps you connect energetically with your soul-aligned clients and community members, strengthening the field of sacred circle around your business.

Sacred Intention: To create and strengthen energetic connections with those who are truly yours to serve, following Mary Magdalene's model of gathering her sacred circle.

What You'll Need:

- A quiet, undisturbed space
- A circle of string, ribbon, or flowers to sit within
- Candle
- Rose oil or other sacred oil
- Images or symbols representing your ideal community (optional)

The Ceremony

1. *Creating Sacred Space*

- Arrange your string, ribbon, or flowers in a circle around you
- Light your candle in the center of your circle, saying: *"I illuminate the sacred circle of my business community."*
- Place a drop of oil on your heart center, saying: *"I open to soul-level connection beyond strategic networking."*
- Take three deep breaths, centering yourself in sacred presence.

2. *The Upper Room Visualization*

- Close your eyes and visualize yourself in the upper room where Mary Magdalene gathered the early followers
- Feel the quality of deep, authentic connection in this space—not networking but true soul recognition
- Sense Mary Magdalene's presence beside you, guiding you in the art of sacred circle

- Ask her: "Who are the souls truly aligned with my work? Who belongs in my sacred circle?"
- Allow images, feelings, or knowing about your soul-aligned community to emerge

3. *The Soul-Client Invitation*

- From this upper room space, begin to energetically invite your aligned clients and community
- You don't need to see specific faces; simply feel the quality of those who resonate with your unique medicine
- As each soul presence joins your circle, welcome them with: "I recognize you. Your soul knows mine. We are meant to journey together."
- Continue until you feel your circle is complete

4. *The Sacred Circle Activation*

- With your community gathered energetically around you, place both hands over your heart
- Visualize golden light emanating from your heart, creating a luminous thread that connects you with each person in your circle
- See this connection as mutual rather than hierarchical—a sacred exchange rather than a one-way delivery
- Feel the power that comes from depth of connection rather than breadth of reach
- Declare: "This is my sacred circle. These are the souls I am truly meant to serve. I release the exhaustion of reaching everyone and embrace the power of connecting deeply with those who recognize my medicine."

5. *The Practical Guidance Reception*

- Still seated within your circle, ask Mary Magdalene: "How can I more effectively gather and serve my sacred circle in practical terms?"

- Listen deeply for guidance about specific actions, channels, or approaches that will attract and nurture your aligned community
- This guidance often contradicts conventional marketing wisdom, so listen without judgment
- When the guidance feels complete, say: *"I receive this wisdom about nurturing my sacred circle."*

6. Closing the Meditation

- Thank each soul presence in your circle, saying: *"Until we meet in physical form, our connection remains in sacred space."*
- Thank Mary Magdalene for her guidance in the way of sacred circle
- Place your hands on the physical circle around you, saying: *"This sacred circle now extends into my business. I trust resonance over reach. I prioritize depth over breadth. I cultivate community through authentic connection rather than strategic networking."*
- Take three deep breaths, feeling this intention fully integrated
- Blow out your candle, knowing the sacred circle remains energetically activated

Perform this meditation monthly to strengthen your energetic connection with your soul-aligned community or whenever you feel tempted to fall back into exhausting networking patterns.

Creating Your Soul-Aligned Business Collective

When you shift from audience-building to sacred circle creation, your approach to gathering your business community transforms. Here are practical ways to cultivate your soul-aligned collective:

Soul Recognition Gatherings

Instead of networking events focused on collecting contacts, create or attend gatherings designed for depth of connection. These might be intimate dinners, sacred circles, or retreats where genuine sharing is prioritized over business card exchanges.

A friend transformed her business by hosting monthly "Tea & Truth" gatherings for just eight women at a time. These intimate events created such profound connections that participants naturally became clients, collaborators, and referral sources, without any "selling" involved.

Resonance-Based Content

Rather than creating content designed to appeal to the widest possible audience, focus on expressing your most authentic truth, even if it resonates with fewer people initially.

Ask yourself: "What truth is living in me that needs expression?" rather than "What will get the most engagement?" When you create from this place, your content naturally magnetizes those who are meant to be in your circle.

Sacred Space Online

Even virtual spaces can be sacred when approached with intention. Consider:

- Private groups or communities with clear agreements about interaction
- Video gatherings with structured space for authentic sharing
- Email communication that feels like personal letters rather than broadcasts

The key is creating containers that foster genuine connection rather than performance or consumption.

Initiation Rather Than Onboarding

When new people enter your business community, treat their arrival as an initiation rather than an onboarding process.

Instead of automated sequences focused on selling, create experiences that:

- Welcome them authentically into your circle
- Invite them to share who they are beyond consumer status
- Offer meaningful connection with you and potentially others
- Create clear context for how your community functions

Sacred Client Selection

Perhaps most revolutionary, recognize that not everyone who wants to work with you belongs in your sacred circle. Develop discernment about who you invite into closer relationship through your offerings.

This is not about exclusivity but about energetic alignment. When you work only with those who truly resonate with your medicine, everyone benefits: you, your aligned clients, and even those who are not aligned (who can find their perfect match elsewhere).

From "Networking" to "Soul Recognition"

If you implement JUST ONE thing from this gateway, let it be this: Stop "networking" and start practicing "soul recognition."

Next time you are at an event or meeting new people online, shift your focus from "How can this person help my business?" to "Do I feel that inexplicable soul recognition with this person?"

This single shift will transform your experience from depleting to energizing, from strategic to sacred, from transactional to transformational.

And THAT, beloved Magdalene Maverick, is the revolutionary path to building a business community that doesn't just support your work but becomes a sacred vessel for collective transformation.

A Love Letter from Mary Magdalene on Sacred Circle

Magdalene sits in meditation, then speaks with profound presence and love

Beloved Circle-Builder,

They have told you that success comes through reaching thousands, through constant visibility, through strategic connections with those who can advance your cause. But I want to share a different truth, the truth I lived when all seemed lost and the movement teetered on collapse.

After the crucifixion, when fear scattered the others, I did not attempt to reach the masses. I gathered those whose souls recognized the truth I carried. In that upper room, we created not a strategy for growth but a container for revelation. And from that intimate circle of authentic connection, a movement spread that would transform the world not through marketing but through the undeniable power of lives transformed.

This is the wisdom I offer you about your business community: The most powerful movements begin not with reaching everyone but deeply connecting with the few who are truly yours to serve. Not with strategic networking but with soul recognition that transcends practical advantage.

Your exhaustion comes not from building community itself but from building it according to principles that contradict the natural law of sacred connection. True community forms not through your striving to reach everyone but through your courage to be so authentically yourself that those who belong in your circle cannot help but recognize you.

This is the way I gathered, not through convincing but through recognizing. Not through reaching but through being. Not through strategy but through truth so powerful it could not be denied even when others attempted to silence it.

Create your business community this way. Release the exhaustion of networking for advantage. Embrace the ease of gathering through resonance. Trust that when you focus on depth rather than breadth, your circle naturally expands not through your effort but through the transformed lives of those you have deeply touched.

The world does not need more strategic networkers, beloved. It needs sacred circle-builders who, like me, have the courage to gather the aligned few when everyone else is scrambling to reach the many.

With eternal recognition of your circle-building power,

—**Mary Magdalene**

"When a woman builds a business community the Magdalene way, she discovers that true influence isn't measured by how many she reaches but by how deeply she connects, for ten thousand lukewarm followers can never create the transformation possible with twelve fully ignited souls."

—***Rose Wilder***

GATEWAY 5

Divine Flow—Honoring Natural Business Rhythms

"She who aligns with the sacred rhythms of creation accomplishes more with ease than others achieve through constant striving."

—*Rose Wilder*

As I write these words about divine flow and natural rhythms, I am sitting in my garden looking at my mountain filled with mature trees in the distance at 5:47 AM, not because some productivity guru told me this was "optimal creative time," but because my body naturally woke with the first light, my creativity flowing like honey. This isn't discipline—it's alignment. This is not hustle, it is not balance, it IS harmony. And that difference, precious sister, changes everything.

Mary Magdalene and the Revolutionary Wisdom of Sacred Cycles

Sister, can we have the most RADICAL conversation about the greatest business lie you have ever been sold? The soul-crushing myth that has you pushing, grinding, and hustling against your own magnificent nature like a salmon swimming upstream in concrete?

I am talking about the absolutely DEVASTATING lie of linear, constant growth.

Have you ever noticed that peculiar, bone-deep disconnect between what your body KNOWS and what business "experts" insist is the only path to success? That grinding exhaustion of trying to maintain the same pace, output, and energy level regardless of your natural rhythms, your monthly cycles, the seasons of your soul? That subtle but persistent inner revolution when you're told to "push through resistance" when every cell in your magnificent being is screaming for rest, reflection, or a completely different approach?

What if I told you that Mary Magdalene—yes, THAT Mary Magdalene—held ancient wisdom about cycles and rhythms that would completely REVOLUTIONIZE how you approach your business, your success, and your entire relationship with productivity?

While much of her story has been fragmented, suppressed, or sanitized by those who feared feminine wisdom, apocryphal texts like the Pistis Sophia reveal her profound understanding of what the ancients called "the turning of the spheres," the cosmic rhythms that govern all creation from galaxies to heartbeats. The Gospel of Mary shows her deep wisdom about the soul's journey through different states and phases. Her connection to lunar cycles, tidal flows, and seasonal wisdom appears repeatedly in mystical traditions that honored her as a keeper of cyclical knowledge.

This was not abstract spiritual philosophy, beloved revolutionary. This was PRACTICAL KNOWLEDGE about how to move through the world in flow and harmony with natural law rather than in constant, exhausting resistance to it.

Consider how PROFOUNDLY DIFFERENT this wisdom is from conventional business approaches:

Modern hustle culture teaches: Linear, constant growth. Always more, always faster, always pushing forward regardless of natural rhythms. It's the ultimate patriarchal fantasy that we can somehow transcend the natural world and its cycles through sheer willpower.

Mary Magdalene understood: ALL of creation moves in cycles, periods of expansion followed naturally by periods of contraction, times of outward expression followed organically by times of inward reflection, seasons of visible growth supported by seasons of invisible development.

This is not some "soft" feminine approach that bypasses ambition or drive. These are the most powerful actions and truths within the divine, fundamental laws that govern EVERYTHING from the divinely created turning of galaxies to the beating of your precious heart to the sustainable success of your revolutionary business.

When My Body Staged a Revolution

Let me share something so deeply personal it still makes my hands shake, the story that revolutionized my entire understanding of divine flow and why, as someone who had to rebuild her entire relationship with safety and control, I understand the terror and magic of surrendering to natural rhythms.

Many years into building my business, I thought I had it all figured out. I found myself once again, mindlessly following many productivity hacks, maintaining consistent output, pushing through fatigue like it was a badge of honor.

Until my body decided to show me a lesson I will never forget.

I had allowed myself to be pulled back into operating my business according to the linear growth model that every expert preaches, every guru demands, and every successful entrepreneur seems to follow. I pushed through exhaustion like it was a badge of honor. I ignored my body's signals as if they were inconvenient interruptions. I forced creativity when it wasn't naturally flowing, like trying to squeeze water from a stone. I maintained the same relentless pace regardless of season, cycle, or what my soul was actually calling for.

The result? Burnout so severe it manifested as serious autoimmune issues that landed me in the hospital, my body literally attacking itself from the stress of constant pushing. Client work that grew increasingly forced, mechanical, and uninspired. A business that was "successful" by every conventional metric but felt completely misaligned with my soul's natural rhythm.

Then came my divine intervention—a health crisis so profound it forced me to STOP ENTIRELY.

In that forced pause, lying in a hospital bed just before 4 AM, unable to work, unable to push, as my body shut down, I was unable to do anything but breathe and be present. In my loneliness and into the unknown filled with fears, as I sobbed, and like an answer to prayer, I felt Yeshua's love and felt that I received Mary Magdalene's wisdom with startling, life-changing clarity:

"All of creation moves in sacred cycles, beloved. The moon waxes and wanes. The tides ebb and flow. The seasons turn in perfect rhythm. Why do you believe your work should be the one exception to this universal law?"

With this revelation came a complete reimagining of my entire business model. I began tracking my natural energy patterns like a scientist studying a precious ecosystem. I designed seasonal rhythms into my offerings rather than maintaining the same exhausting pace year-round. I honored periods of rest as ESSENTIAL to periods of productivity, not lazy interruptions to be overcome.

*Voice becomes bright with wonder.

What happened next DEFIED every piece of conventional business logic I had ever been taught:

My income did not decrease. It stabilized and then grew MORE SUSTAINABLY than ever before. My creative output didn't diminish, it became MORE INSPIRED, aligned, and powerfully effective. My impact didn't lessen, it DEEPENED as my work came from natural flow rather than forced effort. My health returned with such vitality that I felt like I was meeting my body for the first time.

And most importantly, my business began to feel like an organic extension of my being rather than a machine I was constantly struggling to keep running through sheer willpower.

This is the Magdalene way of divine flow: not the exhausting pursuit of constant growth, but the sovereign alignment with natural rhythms that allows your business to breathe, evolve, and flourish according to the same cyclical wisdom that governs all living systems.

Your Body's Sophisticated Guidance System

What if I told you that your body contains the most advanced business planning technology ever created? More sophisticated than any app, more accurate than any strategic framework.

For those who menstruate, your monthly cycle provides an exquisite map for aligning business activities with your natural energetic states:

♀ **Menstrual Phase (Your Inner Winter):** *Like Mary Magdalene in the tomb's darkness* This is your time for deep listening, receiving profound downloads, and visioning from the depths. Your intuition is at its PEAK during this phase—the veil between worlds is thinnest, and your access to divine guidance is strongest.

- ALIGN WITH: Strategic planning, intuitive business guidance, rest, profound reflection
- AVOID: Public speaking, high-stakes sales conversations, launch activities, anything requiring external energy
- MAGDALENE WISDOM: *"The darkness before dawn is necessary for the deepest revelations to emerge. Honor the sacred pause."*

One of my clients completely transformed her business by protecting her menstrual phase as sacred "download time." She now reserves her most important strategic decisions for this phase, when her intuitive wisdom is strongest. "The guidance I receive during my inner winter has been absolutely GAME-CHANGING," she shared with awe. "It's like having direct access to divine business intelligence in a way that never happens during other phases."

♀ **Follicular Phase (Your Inner Spring):** *Like Mary Magdalene proclaiming the resurrection* As energy rises like sap in trees, this is your time for new beginnings, fresh initiatives, and outward expression. Your creativity and optimism naturally expand like flowers reaching toward the sun.

- ALIGN WITH: Launching new offerings, visibility activities, creative development, planting seeds
- NURTURE: New ideas, fresh approaches, innovative solutions
- MAGDALENE WISDOM: *"From the tomb emerges new life, unstoppable in its becoming. Trust the natural emergence."*

♀ **Ovulatory Phase (Your Inner Summer):** *Like Mary Magdalene teaching her disciples* At your energetic peak, radiating magnetic presence, this is your time for connection, collaboration, and maximum visibility. Your communication skills and charismatic presence are naturally heightened.

- ALIGN WITH: Speaking engagements, networking events, client enrollment conversations, video creation
- LEVERAGE: Your natural magnetism, verbal fluency, and collaborative energy
- MAGDALENE WISDOM: *"Share your light at its brightest so others may recognize and remember their own brilliance."*

♀ **Luteal Phase (Your Inner Autumn):** *Like Mary Magdalene completing sacred preparations* As energy begins to naturally wane, this is your time for completion, evaluation, and turning inward. Your analytical skills and attention to detail reach their peak.

- ALIGN WITH: Administrative tasks, client delivery, project completion, evaluation, and refinement
- HONOR: The need for increased structure, clear boundaries, and less social energy
- MAGDALENE WISDOM: "The harvest comes before the rest. Complete what must be completed with grace and thoroughness."

For those who no longer menstruate or wish to connect with universal rhythms, the moon phases offer a similar cyclical template, as do the earth's seasons themselves. The key is recognizing that you are not meant to operate at the same energy level, pace, or focus every single day of the month or year.

When you align your business activities with these natural rhythms instead of fighting against them, you stop exhausting yourself swimming upstream and start flowing with your divine design. This is not accommodating weakness—it is strategic brilliance.

The Natural Business Calendar

Instead of forcing your business into arbitrary quarterly targets, what if you organized around the wisdom of natural seasons?

♡ **Winter Business Season (December-February):** *The Sacred Gestation* Honor this as your season of rest, deep reflection, and inner preparation. Focus on strategic visioning, soul replenishment, and foundation-setting rather than major launches or external expansion. This is when your clearest insights download, when your most authentic vision emerges from fertile darkness.

*Points to the north point of the circle.

MAGDALENE WISDOM: "The seed beneath the snow knows exactly when to emerge, not by force but by attunement to the warming earth. Trust the invisible preparation happening in the depths."

❦ **Spring Business Season (March-May):** *The Sacred Awakening* Honor this as your season of new growth, fresh initiation, and rising energy. Focus on launching new offerings, expanding visibility, and planting seeds for the year's harvest. Your creativity flows naturally, enthusiasm builds organically, and new possibilities want to emerge through you.

Moves finger to the east point with building excitement.

MAGDALENE WISDOM: "New life comes not through striving but through surrender to the natural impulse of becoming. Allow what wants to be born to move through you."

❦ **Summer Business Season (June-August):** *The Sacred Abundance* Honor this as your season of full expression, active service, and visible manifestation. Focus on program delivery, deep client connection, and the complete flowering of what you've planted. Your energy peaks naturally, your impact expands organically, and abundance flows like a river in full flood.

Traces to the south point, radiating warmth and fullness.

MAGDALENE WISDOM:: "At the height of your radiance, remember it flows through you from divine source. Shine fully while remaining rooted in sacred ground."

❦ **Autumn Business Season (September-November):** *The Sacred Harvest* Honor this as your season of completion, grateful celebration, and conscious preparation for rest. Focus on gathering testimonials, integrating wisdom, and completing cycles before winter's regenerative pause. This is when you distill the gold from your experiences and prepare for the next spiral of growth.

Completes the circle at the west point.

MAGDALENE WISDOM:: "The falling leaf does not resist its journey to nourish the roots. Complete with grace, knowing every ending makes new beginnings possible."

This cyclical approach aligns you with creation's fundamental rhythms rather than arbitrary calendar divisions, creating sustainable success that honors natural intelligence.

One client revolutionized her approach using seasonal wisdom. Instead of forcing launches year-round, she creates one major offering each spring, delivers with full presence during summer, integrates wisdom in autumn, and rests deeply in winter.

"For the first time in eight years, I'm not chronically exhausted," she shared. "My clients receive profound transformation because I'm fully resourced when I serve them. And surprisingly? My income doubled because my work comes from such authentic alignment."

The Natural Laws of Sustainable Success

Mary Magdalene understood what modern business has forgotten: forced expansion ultimately destroys itself. In nature, growth and rest balance each other perfectly.

Consider these principles that will transform your approach to business:

1. **Sacred Rest Fuels Productivity**—Just as winter prepares the earth for spring's abundance, business rest periods aren't "time off." They are essential preparation for your next expansion. When I honored my need for a complete winter sabbatical, twelve weeks of minimal client work, I returned with clarity and inspiration that led to my most abundant year. It wasn't just more energy; I accessed a deeper level of vision that never would have emerged through constant pushing.
2. **Natural Rhythm Creates Sustainability**—Your business has organic rhythms of energy and rest, creativity and integration. Honor these rather than maintaining constant output, and you create lasting success without burnout. The most successful long-term entrepreneurs I know don't push constantly. They create rhythmic patterns, focused creation followed by integration, intense delivery followed by restoration, that sustain them for decades.

3. **Divine Timing Never Skips Seasons**—You cannot jump from winter's seed to autumn's harvest without spring's growth and summer's flowering. Each phase must be fully honored.
4. **Flow Creates Acceleration, Force Creates Resistance**—When you push against natural rhythms, you create struggle. When you align with divine flow, you accomplish more with less effort and infinitely greater joy.

Recognizing When You Are Fighting Sacred Flow

Let's get courageously honest about the warning signs that you're working against your natural rhythms rather than flowing with the divine intelligence of your business cycles:

Physical Exhaustion Beyond Normal Tiredness

- You are relying on caffeine, sugar, or other stimulants just to maintain basic function throughout the day
- You are experiencing unexplained health issues, especially hormonal imbalances, autoimmune flares, or digestive problems
- You regularly override your body's clear signals requesting rest, different pacing, or nourishment
- Sleep does not restore you anymore; you wake up tired regardless of how many hours you get

Emotional Resistance That Won't Resolve

- You feel persistent resentment about aspects of your business that once brought you joy and excitement
- Your enthusiasm about your work has been replaced by dread, obligation, or mechanical going-through-the-motions
- You find yourself procrastinating on tasks you normally love, feeling heavy about your to-do list
- You feel like you are constantly swimming upstream, fighting against an invisible current

Creativity That Feels Forced and Flat

- Your work feels mechanical rather than inspired, like you're following someone else's formula rather than expressing your authentic genius
- You are recycling old ideas rather than accessing fresh perspectives, innovations, and creative solutions
- The quality of your output has diminished despite working harder and longer than ever
- You feel disconnected from your unique voice and authentic creative expression

Diminishing Returns on Increased Effort

- You are working more hours but seeing fewer results, lower-quality outcomes, or less client satisfaction
- Client transformations aren't as profound or lasting as they used to be when you were more aligned
- Your income has plateaued or decreased despite increased activity, marketing efforts, and time investment
- Opportunities feel forced and struggle-filled rather than flowing naturally into your experience

If these signs are ringing bells of painful recognition, please hear this with all the love in my heart: You are not failing at business, precious one. You are not fundamentally flawed as an entrepreneur. You are simply fighting against your natural flow instead of dancing with the divine intelligence of your own rhythms.

The magnificent news? The moment you begin to align with your cyclical nature and honor divine flow, these symptoms begin to reverse themselves, often with surprising speed and remarkable results.

A beloved client came to me experiencing every single one of these warning signs. Working 60+ hours weekly, she was chronically exhausted, deeply resentful, and seeing steadily diminishing results despite her increased effort and dedication. She felt like she must be fundamentally broken as a business owner.

Together, we explored her natural rhythms and discovered she had been working in complete opposition to her cyclical nature. Her business was energetically in deep autumn, needing completion and integration, yet she was forcing spring launches and summer productivity without honoring the necessary winter rest her entire system desperately craved.

We completely redesigned her business model to align with sacred flow:

- We created seasonal content flows rather than constant posting requirements
- We established clear boundaries around her energy, honoring both productive phases and essential rest periods
- We aligned her program launches with her natural creative cycles rather than arbitrary calendar dates
- We built in sacred pauses for integration, visioning, and regeneration

Ten months later, her life had begun to transform beyond recognition. "I'm working less hours and accomplishing so much more," she shared, radiating a vibrant energy I had never seen in her before. "For the first time ever, my business feels like it's flowing with me rather than constantly draining me. And the most amazing part? My clients are responding positively and engaging with my less frequent yet more aligned offerings, and my income has increased!"

This is the absolute MAGIC of divine flow: more sustainable success, deeper impact, and greater fulfillment through alignment with natural rhythms rather than constant resistance to them.

Your Sacred Rhythms: Daily Practices for Divine Flow

While the big seasonal shifts create the foundational framework, divine flow is ultimately cultivated through daily awareness and micro-adjustments that honor your natural rhythms in each moment. Here are revolutionary practices to integrate into your business rhythm:

Morning Energy Attunement

Before planning your day's activities or forcing yourself through a predetermined schedule, tune into your authentic energetic state:

- Place one hand on your heart and one on your womb (your creative center)
- Take three deep breaths, allowing yourself to honestly feel your true energy level and quality
- Ask: *"What is my natural energy supporting today? What flow am I actually in right now?"*
- Adjust your daily plan to align with this authentic energy rather than fighting against it

I completely revolutionized my productivity and joy by implementing this simple but profound practice. Instead of battling through my predetermined to-do list regardless of my actual capacity, I now ask what my system naturally supports in this moment. Some days that means deep creative work, other days gentle administrative tasks, sometimes nurturing client connection, and occasionally complete rest. By following my energy rather than forcing a rigid agenda, I accomplish more with far less strain and infinitely greater satisfaction.

The Sacred Pivot Practice

Throughout your day, practice conscious pivoting when you encounter resistance or struggle:

- Pause and place your hands on your heart center to reconnect with your inner wisdom
- Ask: *"Is this resistance a sign that timing isn't aligned, or is it simply fear-based avoidance that I need to breathe through?"*
- Listen for the subtle but distinct difference between divine guidance and procrastination patterns
- Follow what your body wisdom reveals with trust and gentle courage

The Three Divine Flow Questions

When making any significant business decision, filter it through these three powerful questions:

1. Is this the natural season for this action in my business and personal cycle?
2. Does this feel like swimming gracefully with the current or struggling against it?
3. Am I moving from divine guidance and inner knowing, or from fear of missing out and external pressure?

These questions create a powerful discernment filter for aligning with sacred flow in every choice you make.

Cyclical Awareness Practice

Develop ongoing awareness of the larger cycles operating in your business and life:

- Keep visual reminders of the current moon phase and earth season where you can see them daily
- Note where you are in your personal monthly cycle (if applicable) and honor that energy
- Recognize what energetic season your business is actually in, regardless of the calendar
- Honor the specific gifts, challenges, and requirements of each phase

The Evening Integration Ritual

End each business day with a brief flow integration practice:

- Acknowledge what phase of your larger business cycle you're currently experiencing
- Celebrate moments when you honored divine flow today instead of forcing outcomes

- Notice any attempts to push against natural rhythm that created struggle or depletion
- Set gentle intention to flow with your sacred timing even more fully tomorrow

These daily practices strengthen your connection to cyclical wisdom while creating clear energetic boundaries between aligned action and forced effort. Over time, they become second nature—an intuitive dance with your own divine flow that creates sustainable success, deep fulfillment, and profound alignment.

Ceremony: Blessing All Seasons of Your Sacred Business

Create a magnificent altar with seasonal elements from nature's wisdom

This powerful ceremony honors both the expansion and contraction phases of your business cycle, helping you embrace resting phases as equally valuable and necessary to active growth periods.

Sacred Intention: To ceremonially honor all phases of your business cycle, release judgment about necessary contraction periods, and align completely with the wisdom of natural rhythms in your work and life.

What You'll Need:

- A flowering plant or fresh flowers in full, vibrant bloom
- Seeds from the same plant type (or any seeds that call to your heart)
- Rich, dark soil in a beautiful ceramic bowl
- Pure water in a sacred vessel
- Items representing all four seasons (crystals, leaves, shells, feathers, stones)
- A white or gold candle for illumination
- Journal and pen for receiving guidance
- Music that invites natural cycles and seasonal flow (optional)

The Sacred Ceremony:

1. *Opening the Sacred Container*

   - Light your candle with reverent intention: *"I create sacred space to honor the complete natural cycles of my business—both blooming and resting, both expansion and contraction, both visible growth and invisible development."*
   - Take three deep breaths, feeling yourself fully present in this transformative moment
   - Place your hands over your creative center and feel the wisdom of cycles encoded within your own body

2. *Honoring the Magnificent Bloom*

   - Focus your attention lovingly on the flowering plant or fresh blooms
   - Touch the petals gently, appreciating their beauty, vibrancy, and full expression
   - Say with deep reverence: *"I honor the blooming phases of my business, the launches, the visible growth, the active expression, the abundant manifestation. I celebrate these times of expansion and recognize their beauty, power, and sacred value in the cycle of creation."*
   - In your journal, write down all aspects of your business currently in bloom or full expression
   - Express profound gratitude: *"I am grateful for these beautiful manifestations of my work flowering brilliantly in the world."*

3. *Honoring the Sacred Preparation*

   - Now focus on the seeds and rich soil with equal reverence and appreciation
   - Hold several seeds in your palm, feeling their incredible dormant potential
   - Say with deep honoring: *"I honor the resting phases of my business— the planning, the invisible development, the necessary integration, the essential replenishment. I celebrate these times of apparent dormancy and recognize their absolute necessity and profound sacred value."*

- Plant the seeds in the soil with loving intention: *"Just as these seeds require darkness, stillness, and time to develop strong, deep roots, my business requires periods of rest and reflection to develop sustainable foundations for lasting, meaningful success."*
- Pour water gently onto the planted seeds: *"I nourish the invisible growth with my conscious attention and loving care, knowing that what develops beneath the surface will eventually emerge in perfect divine timing."*
- Write down all aspects of your business currently in development, rest, or integration phase
- Express equal gratitude for these developing aspects with the same enthusiasm

4. *The Complete Cycle Blessing*

- Stand before your seasonal altar with arms extended in profound sacred blessing
- Speak this blessing over your business with complete conviction and love:

"I bless the complete, sacred cycle of my business—The expansion and the contraction, The blooming and the resting, The visible growth and the invisible development, The active seasons and the receptive seasons.

Like Mary Magdalene who understood the turning of divine timing, I recognize that all phases are necessary, valuable, and holy. I release all judgment about periods of apparent dormancy, knowing they are essential preparation for the next magnificent blooming.

I bless the winter of my business, when ideas germinate in fertile darkness and sacred silence. I bless the spring of my business, when new initiatives emerge with fresh energy and natural enthusiasm. I bless the summer of my business, when offerings reach their full, vibrant expression and abundant fruition. I bless the autumn of my business, when completion and integration prepare the fertile ground for the next cycle.

I honor the natural rhythm of growth and rest, of giving and receiving, of expression and reflection, of doing and being.

I commit to flowing with these sacred cycles rather than fighting against natural wisdom. I trust that honoring all phases creates more sustainable success than forcing constant blooming without essential restoration.

This business flows in divine rhythm, Honoring all seasons as equally valuable and necessary. My success is sustainable because it follows natural law. And so it is."

5. Personal Divine Flow Commitment

- Create a specific, heartfelt commitment to honor your current business season
- Write this commitment in your journal with your full signature
- Say aloud: *"I commit to the profound wisdom of sacred cycles in my business and life."*

6. Closing the Sacred Space

- Place one hand on the blooming plant and one on the planted seeds
- Feel the deep, profound connection between these different phases of the same miraculous life cycle
- Express heartfelt gratitude to Mary Magdalene for her guidance in cyclical wisdom
- Say: *"It is complete. My life and business are now fully aligned with divine flow. All phases are honored as sacred and necessary. Perfect timing is trusted completely. And so it is."*

Keep both your flowering plant and your seed pot visible in your workspace as daily reminders of the complete cycle necessary for truly sustainable business success.

Divine Flow—Honoring Natural Business Rhythms

A Sacred Message from Mary Magdalene on Divine Flow

Mary Magdalene appears in meditation, emanating the profound peace of someone who trusts completely in divine orchestration and natural timing.

My Beloved Daughter of Sacred Flow,

In the stories they tell of me, you rarely hear of how intimately I understood the turning of the spheres, the sacred rhythms that govern all creation from the movement of distant stars to the beating of your precious, powerful heart. They speak of my devotion and my witness, but seldom of how I moved through the world in complete harmony with natural cycles rather than in exhausting resistance to them.

This profound wisdom I now share with you, treasured one: There is a rhythm to all creation that cannot be forced, rushed, or manipulated through human will, strategy, or relentless effort. Just as the moon moves through her necessary phases without apology, just as the earth honors her distinct seasons without hurrying, your business has natural cycles of expansion and contraction, of blooming and dormancy, of outward expression and inward reflection.

The world will tell you that success means constant growth, relentless productivity, continuous visibility, and never-ending hustle. But I have watched civilizations rise and fall through my eternal perspective, and I tell you this unchanging truth: What endures is not what forces constant expansion but what honors the sacred wisdom of natural cycles.

Your periods of rest are not failure but essential preparation for your next emergence. Your times of reflection are not wasted but crucial for developing deeper roots and clearer vision. Your phases of integration are not stagnation but necessary consolidation before your next beautiful, powerful expansion.

When you align your business with these natural rhythms, you discover that you accomplish more through divine flow than others achieve through constant forcing. You create more sustainable success through honoring all phases than those who exhaust themselves pushing against natural contraction. You build something that lasts because it follows the laws that govern all lasting creation.

This is the forgotten wisdom I embodied: the understanding that divine flow creates more powerful results than human force ever could. That working with natural cycles amplifies your impact rather than diminishing it. That honoring the necessary winter of your business creates a more vibrant, sustainable spring than trying to maintain perpetual summer through willpower alone.

Trust the rhythm of your business as you would trust the turning of the seasons. Honor the phase you're in rather than rushing toward the next. Know that in surrendering to divine flow, you align with the very forces that govern creation itself.

Your success becomes not just profitable but sustainable, not just impactful but enduring, because it flows with rather than against the fundamental laws of life itself.

With infinite wisdom from beyond time and complete trust in your divine flow,

—Mary Magdalene

Divine Flow—Honoring Natural Business Rhythms

"She who honors all seasons of her business—winter's sacred rest, spring's joyful emergence, summer's abundant flowering, and autumn's grateful completion—creates success that not only flourishes but endures for generations, for she works with the forces of creation rather than against them."

—Rose Wilder

GATEWAY 6

Sacred Service—Giving Without Depletion

"True service is not measured by how much you give, but by how full you remain in the giving."

—Rose Wilder

The Sacred Art of Sustainable Service

Oh, beloved, let me start with a truth bomb that may rattle some cages: The most dangerous lie spiritual women have been fed? That depletion equals devotion. That your worth is measured by how empty you become in service of others.

I am here to obliterate that myth completely, and trust me, as someone who has walked through abduction and been held captive, to come back from it all, I know a thing or two about recognizing dangerous lies disguised as spiritual truth.

Have you ever felt that bone-deep exhaustion that comes not just from working hard, but from emptying your very essence into your business? That peculiar energetic anemia when you've given far beyond your capacity? That quiet resentment bubbling up when you have poured out so much there is nothing left for yourself, and then the guilt because "good spiritual women should not feel resentful"?

Sister, you are singing my song. And Mary Magdalene? She has got the revolutionary remedy we have all been desperately seeking.

For centuries—CENTURIES—feminine wisdom keepers have been spoon-fed this toxic narrative that service means sacrifice. That boundaries are selfish. That self-care is indulgent. This distortion has led countless spiritual entrepreneurs down a path of burnout and diminished impact, the very opposite of the sacred service they longed to offer.

But here is where it gets juicy, where the Magdalene Maverick in me starts dancing with rebellious joy: Scripture gives us a completely different model. Let's get inspired by Luke 8:3, which tells us that Mary Magdalene "provided for them out of her resources."

Notice the critical distinction, beautiful one: she gave from what she *had*, not from what she did not have. She served from abundance, not emptiness. She gave from overflow, not depletion. She was the original anti-hustle entrepreneur, serving sustainably while everyone else was burning themselves to the ground!

This is the sacred art of sustainable service: understanding that your greatest gift to the world is not your exhaustion but your embodied wholeness. Not your depletion but your divine overflow. Not your martyrdom but your magnificent, sustained presence.

The Sacred Mathematics of Sustainable Service

Mary Magdalene understood something that modern spiritual entrepreneurs, caught up in the toxic productivity culture that even infiltrates our sacred work, often forget: there is sacred mathematics to sustainable service that flies directly in the face of hustle culture.

Here is the equation that changed everything for me (and will revolutionize your approach, too):

Your impact equals the depth of your service multiplied by how long you can sustain it.

Let that marinate for a moment, gorgeous.

When you serve from depletion, you might give 100% in the moment, but you can only sustain it briefly before burnout forces you to stop entirely. It's like setting yourself on fire to provide warmth, dramatic, but ultimately destructive and unsustainable.

When you serve from overflow, you give a sustainable 80% consistently, creating exponentially greater impact over time. It's like becoming a steady hearth fire that warms countless souls across decades rather than a spectacular blaze that burns out quickly.

This sacred mathematics applies to every aspect of your business: your client load, session boundaries, pricing structure, and offering design. The most profound service you can offer is not momentary over-giving but sustainable presence that continues to nourish others year after year.

This is how Mary Magdalene served. Not through momentary martyrdom but through sustained, sovereign offering of her resources, wisdom, and presence. She was playing the long game of transformation, honey, and we need to learn from her wisdom.

The Revolutionary Truth About Boundaries as Divine Containers

Here is where my Magdalene Maverick heart gets absolutely electric with excitement: In the authentic Magdalene tradition, boundaries are not obstacles to service. They are sacred containers that make profound service possible!

This is such a radical departure from what we've been taught. We have been conditioned to believe that boundaries are walls that separate us from those we serve, that they are somehow "unspiritual" or "unloving." But listen closely, beautiful revolutionary: They are not walls that separate you from those you serve but vessels that hold the transformative power of your work.

Let me paint you a picture that will shift everything: Consider Mary Magdalene's alabaster jar. It was precisely the container, the boundary, that preserved the precious spikenard until the perfect moment for offering. Without that container, the oil would have dissipated long before it could fulfill its sacred purpose.

Your boundaries serve the same function, and this is where the magic happens:

- They don't limit your impact; they concentrate it like a laser beam
- They don't diminish your giving; they ensure its potency and purity
- They don't reduce your service; they guarantee its sustainability
- They don't make you less loving; they make your love more intentional and powerful

Let me share a story that illustrates this beautifully: One of my clients, a brilliant healer, found herself in tears after years of boundary-less service had left her depleted and resentful. "I started this work because I love helping people," she confessed, "but now I dread client calls. I feel like a fraud. How can I help others heal when I'm so broken inside?"

This broke my heart because I recognized the pattern immediately. Together, we explored the Magdalene model: clear session boundaries, specific communication channels, and offerings that expressed her unique medicine without endless customization that drained her life force.

Six months later, her practice had completely transformed. Not only had her well-being returned in full vibrancy, but her clients were experiencing more profound results than ever before.

"The most surprising part," she shared with tears of joy rather than exhaustion, "is that my clients actually respect me more now that I have clear boundaries. They value the container I create because it holds their transformation more powerfully than my boundary-less availability ever did."

This is the paradox of sacred boundaries that the Magdalene Maverick in me absolutely loves: they do not limit your service; they amplify it.

They don't constrain your impact; they sustain it. They do not separate you from those you serve; they create the sacred container where true transformation occurs.

The Sovereign Vessel of Your Energy: Reclaiming Your Power

As spiritual entrepreneurs, especially those of us with big, generous hearts and natural empathic gifts, many of us struggle with boundaries because we feel others' pain so acutely that drawing any line feels like withholding help. I get it, sister. I really do.

Yet here is where Mary Magdalene offers a revolutionary perspective that will set you free: *Your energy is a sovereign vessel entrusted to your stewardship, not an unlimited public resource to be drained by anyone with a request.*

Read that again. Let it sink into your bones.

As someone who survived abduction and trauma, I learned this lesson the hardest way possible: when you do not protect your energy vessel, others will drain it without conscience. But when you honor it as sacred, you create space for genuine transformation, both yours and theirs.

Consider how Mary Magdalene served from her resources, not from anticipated future earnings (the entrepreneur's trap!), not from energetic debt, not from martyred self-sacrifice, but from what she actually possessed. This reflects profound wisdom about energetic sovereignty that every modern Magdalene must master.

Your energy vessel has three sacred levels:

- **Essential Reserves:** The sacred foundation that must remain untouched to maintain your well-being. This is your life force, your core vitality, your non-negotiable inner sanctuary
- **Personal Replenishment:** The middle level that nourishes your own growth, joy, creativity, and dreams. This is where you fill yourself up, pursue your passions, and tend to your own evolution

- **Divine Overflow:** The abundant top level from which you serve others. This is the generous surplus that flows naturally when the other levels are honored

When you serve only from divine overflow, you maintain the integrity of your entire vessel. When you dip into essential reserves, you compromise not just your well-being but your capacity to serve sustainably. It's like trying to water a garden with the last drops in your own water bottle... nobody wins.

Revolutionary Practices for Sustainable Service

Mary Magdalene's model gives us practical wisdom for serving powerfully without depletion. These are not just pretty concepts, sister. They are battle-tested strategies that will transform how you show up in your business:

The Sacred Container Practice

For every offering, create clear boundaries that feel both loving and firm:

Time Containers:

- Specific start and end times honored without exception (yes, even when someone is "just about to have a breakthrough")
- Sacred transition time between sessions to reset your energy
- Rhythmic service patterns that honor your natural cycles (Hello, menstrual wisdom!)

Communication Containers:

- Clear channels with stated response timeframes
- Boundaries around after-hours availability
- Explicit inclusions and exclusions to prevent scope creep

Energy Containers:

- Pre-session rituals to center yourself
- Post-session practices to release absorbed energies
- Weekly restoration activities that fill your cup

The Divine Overflow Check

Before saying yes to any request, pause and ask these revolutionary questions:

- Can I offer this from my overflow, or would it require dipping into my essential reserves?
- Will this energize me or deplete me? (Trust your body's wisdom here!)
- Is this aligned with my unique medicine, or am I trying to be everything to everyone?
- What would Mary Magdalene do? Serve from abundance or sacrifice from emptiness?

The Sacred No Practice

Learn to say no as a spiritual practice, recognizing that:

- Every no to what depletes you is a sacred yes to sustainable service
- Every boundary you maintain models healthy limits for others
- Every request you lovingly redirect serves the client better by connecting them with their perfect match
- Your no creates space for your magnificent yes

The Replenishment Ceremony

Create sacred practices to refill your vessel after giving:

Immediate Reset:

- Post-session cleansing breath work
- Energy clearing visualization
- Gratitude practice for the exchange

Weekly Restoration:

- Soul-nourishing activities that have nothing to do with work
- Time in nature to reconnect with the earth's abundance
- Creative expression that feeds your spirit

Seasonal Renewal:

- Retreats that nourish your essential reserves
- Vision quests that reconnect you with your purpose
- Deep rest that isn't earned but given as sacred gift

The Magdalene Abundance-Based Service Transmission

This is not just meditation, gorgeous. It is a complete rewiring of how you approach service. I have seen this ceremony transform burned-out healers into sustainably powerful change-makers who serve from overflow rather than emptiness.

Sacred Intention: To embody Mary Magdalene's wisdom of serving from abundance rather than depletion, transforming your entire relationship with giving and receiving.

What You'll Need:

- A comfortable, sacred space where you won't be interrupted
- A beautiful vessel filled with clean water (representing your resources)

Sacred Service—Giving Without Depletion

- A smaller empty vessel (representing those you serve)
- Rose oil or sacred oil that calls to your heart
- A white or red candle
- Your journal for capturing insights

The Ceremony

Creating Sacred Space:

- Light your candle with intention, saying: *"I illuminate the path of sustainable service in the footsteps of Mary Magdalene."*
- Add a few drops of oil to your filled vessel, feeling the sacred blessing as you say: *"I consecrate these resources as abundant, sacred, and sustainably renewable."*
- Take three deep breaths, feeling yourself dropping into sacred presence. This is your time, your space, your sacred transformation.

The Depletion Recognition (With Compassion)

Close your eyes and bring to mind, without judgment and only with loving recognition, times when you've served from depletion. Feel in your body the sensation of giving beyond your capacity.

Acknowledge the patterns of over-giving in your business:

- Extending sessions beyond their sacred container
- Being available at all hours like an energetic 24/7 emergency room
- Customizing endlessly until you lose sight of your own offerings
- Undercharging because you have been taught that spiritual work shouldn't be profitable

As you recognize each pattern, place your hand on your heart and say with deep compassion: *"I acknowledge how I've tried to serve from emptiness rather than fullness, and I forgive myself for not knowing a better way."*

Feel how this depletion-based service affects both you and those you aim to serve. Notice how it actually diminishes rather than enhances your impact.

The Mary Magdalene Transmission

Now, visualize Mary Magdalene standing before you in all her radiant wisdom and power. See her not as the diminished figure patriarchy created, but as the abundant, sovereign woman she truly was.

Feel her serving abundantly yet sovereignly from her resources, never from depletion, always from overflow. Notice how this makes her MORE powerful, not less.

Feel her placing her hands on your shoulders, transmitting directly into your energy field the understanding that true service flows from fullness, not emptiness.

Hear her words resonating in every cell: *"Beloved sister, your greatest service comes not from your exhaustion but from your overflow. Fill your vessel first, then serve from that sacred abundance. This is not selfish, this is sustainable. This is not less spiritual, this is more powerful."*

Receive this transmission completely, feeling it transforming your entire nervous system's approach to service.

The Sacred Mathematics Visualization

Open your eyes and look at your filled vessel with new appreciation.

Pour a small amount into the empty vessel, saying with conviction: *"This represents sustainable service from overflow... generous, but not depleting."*

Notice that you still have plenty remaining in your primary vessel. This is the key!

Say with growing excitement: *"I can continue serving from this abundance indefinitely, creating exponentially greater impact over time than if I emptied my vessel completely in one dramatic gesture."*

Refill your primary vessel, saying: *"And as I prioritize replenishment, my capacity to serve sustainably increases rather than diminishes."*

The Boundary Blessing

Hold both vessels in your hands, feeling their weight and significance.

Say with fierce love: *"I bless the sacred boundaries that contain my service. Like Mary Magdalene's alabaster jar, these boundaries don't limit my offering but preserve its potency until the perfect moment for giving."*

Visualize your entire business surrounded by a luminous, protective container that concentrates rather than constrains your impact.

Say with growing power: *"My boundaries are not obstacles to service but sacred vessels that make profound service possible. They are expressions of love, not barriers to it."*

The Sustainable Service Commitment

Place both hands over your heart and feel the complete shift from depletion-based to abundance-based service happening at the cellular level.

Speak your sacred commitment aloud:

"I, [your name], commit to serving from divine overflow rather than depletion. Like Mary Magdalene who provided from her resources, I give from what I have, not from what I don't have. I honor my boundaries as sacred containers for transformation. I recognize that my sustainable presence creates infinitely greater impact than momentary sacrifice followed by inevitable burnout. I commit to filling my vessel first, then serving others from that blessed abundance. I trust that this way of serving honors both me and those I'm here to help. I am a Magdalene Maverick, and I serve sustainably. And so it is."

Closing the Sacred Circle

Pour a final small amount from your filled vessel to your empty one, saying with deep knowing: *"From fullness, not emptiness. From sovereignty, not sacrifice. From sustainability, not depletion. This is the Magdalene way."*

Take three deep breaths, feeling this new model of service fully integrated into your being.

Blow out your candle, saying: *"It is done. I serve from abundance. My impact is sustainable. I am a vessel of lasting transformation. And so it is."*

Integration: Practice this ritual monthly or whenever you notice yourself slipping back into patterns of depletion-based service. Keep your vessels as sacred reminders of your new commitment.

Consecrating Your Sacred Boundaries: The Magdalene Maverick Method

Creating clear, compassionate boundaries that enhance rather than limit your service is an essential practice for every modern Magdalene. This isn't about being cold or uncaring. It's about being so deeply caring that you create sustainable structures for lasting transformation.

Define Your Sacred Time Container

Session Boundaries:

- Set specific session lengths that honor both transformation and your energy (and stick to them like your business life depends on it, because it does!)
- Establish sacred work hours that protect your personal life from constant intrusion
- Determine your ideal client load per day/week that ensures quality service without energetic bankruptcy
- Create buffer time between sessions for integration, reset, and transition

Personal Time Protection:

- Designate technology-free zones and times
- Protect your weekends and holidays as sacred restoration time
- Honor your body's natural rhythms (early bird or night owl; work WITH your energy, not against it)

Design Your Sacred Energy Container

Soul-Aligned Client Recognition:

- Identify the qualities of clients who energize rather than drain you
- Recognize the red flags that signal energy vampires disguised as "ideal clients"
- Trust your gut when someone feels "off." Your intuition is your greatest business asset
- Create intake processes that attract aligned souls and repel energy drains

Zone of Genius Clarity:

- Clarify the specific types of work that fall within your unique medicine
- Recognize the signs that tell you when to refer someone elsewhere
- Stop trying to be everything to everyone (You're not Amazon, honey!)
- Develop a network of colleagues for referrals

Establish Your Sacred Offering Container

Clear Inclusions and Boundaries:

- Define the specific components included in each offering with crystal clarity
- Set loving but firm parameters around customization
- Identify the types of requests you gracefully redirect
- Create language that maintains the integrity of your offerings while honoring the client

Value Protection:

- Price your offerings based on transformation, not time
- Resist the urge to constantly add "free bonuses" that dilute your boundaries
- Maintain consistency in your offerings to avoid decision fatigue

Create Your Sacred Communication Container

Channel Clarity:

- Specify exactly how clients can reach you (email, portal, phone, etc.)
- Set clear response timeframes for each channel
- Establish firm boundaries around emergency contact (define what constitutes a true emergency)
- Create simple, loving language to communicate these parameters

Energy Management:

- Batch similar communications
- Use templates for common questions
- Set specific times for checking and responding to messages
- Protect your creative time from constant interruption

Honor Your Sacred Exchange Container

Value-Based Pricing:

- Set rates that reflect the true value of the transformation you facilitate
- Price for sustainability, not just immediate sales
- Clarify the specific circumstances (if any) for adjusted rates
- Define what constitutes "included" versus additional investment

Exchange Integrity:

- Create clear language about value exchange that honors both parties
- Resist the urge to constantly discount or add freebies
- Understand that your price is a boundary that attracts aligned clients

Compassionate Boundary Language: The Art of Loving Firmness

HOW you express your boundaries is as crucial as HAVING them. This is where the magic happens, maintaining your sacred containers while keeping your heart open and your communication warm.

Session Management

When Sessions Run Over: "We have reached the end of our sacred time together, and I want to honor both the beautiful container we've created for your transformation and my commitment to be fully present for all my clients. Let's either schedule another session to continue this important work, or let's find a powerful way to bring closure to today's exploration. What feels most aligned for you?"

When Clients Want to Extend Last-Minute: "I can feel how much momentum you have right now, and that's beautiful! To give this the full attention and energy it deserves, let's schedule a dedicated session rather than trying to squeeze it into the end of today's container. When would work best for you?"

Scope and Offering Protection

When Requests Fall Outside Your Offerings: "What you're asking for is so important, and I can see how much it means to you. This particular request falls outside the scope of this offering, but I'd love to explore how we might address it through [appropriate offering], or I can recommend a colleague who specializes in exactly this area. Let me think about the best way to support you here."

When Asked for Extensive Customization: "I've designed this offering very thoughtfully to create maximum transformation within a sustainable container. While I can't customize extensively (as that would compromise the integrity of the work for everyone), I can [small adaptation if appropriate] or guide you toward the offering that might be a better fit for your specific needs."

Communication Boundaries

When Contacted Outside Hours: "Thank you for reaching out. I can feel the importance of what you are sharing. I have received your message and will respond during my dedicated client communication hours on [specific day/time]. This boundary allows me to show up completely present and resourced when I do respond, which serves you better than a scattered, depleted response. I'm holding space for you in the meantime."

For Non-Emergency After-Hours Contact: "I honor the urgency you're feeling, and I want to give your situation the full attention it deserves. Unless this is a true emergency [define what you consider emergency], I'll respond during my next communication window on [time]. This allows me to be fully present with your needs rather than responding from depletion."

Financial Boundaries

When Asked for Discounts: "I have thoughtfully established my investment levels to reflect the depth of transformation this work facilitates and to ensure I can continue serving sustainably and wholeheartedly. While I'm unable to adjust my rates, I can offer [payment plan/entry-level offering/partial exchange scholarship if available] as an alternative way for us to work together. What feels most aligned for your situation?"

When Feeling Pressured to Lower Prices: "I understand investment is a consideration, and I honor whatever decision feels right for you. My rates reflect not just my time, but the years of training, the depth of transformation facilitated, and my commitment to sustainable service. I trust that the right-aligned clients will recognize this value, and there's no pressure for that to be everyone."

Energy Management

When Feeling Depleted: "I notice I am approaching my energetic capacity, and rather than serve you from depletion (which wouldn't honor either of us), I need to pause and replenish so I can continue showing up powerfully. Let's [reschedule/take a break/address this in our next session]. This isn't personal, it's professional energetic management."

When Clients Become Emotionally Demanding: "I can see you are in a lot of pain right now, and I want to support you. I also want to make sure I can continue being a stable, grounded presence for you, which means I need to maintain some energetic boundaries around our work together. Let's explore how to get you the level of support you need while keeping our work sustainable."

The Sacred Art of Receiving: Revolution in Reverse

Here's where I get to share one of the most revolutionary truths about sustainable service, and honey, this one might make you squirm a little because it flies in the face of everything we've been taught about feminine "virtue."

Receiving is as sacred as giving.

Let that land. Let it challenge every martyrdom story you've been told.

Mary Magdalene didn't just give to the ministry; she also received. The gospels tell us she was healed by Yeshua before she became a supporter of the ministry. She received before she gave. She allowed herself to be filled before offering from her overflow.

For many spiritual entrepreneurs, particularly women, receiving can feel more challenging than giving. We've been conditioned to believe that constantly giving while refusing to receive is somehow more spiritual, more feminine, more worthy.

But this is another lie designed to keep us depleted and controllable.

True sustainability requires a sacred balance of giving AND receiving. Just as nature inhales and exhales, contracts and expands, rests and grows, your service must include both giving to others and receiving what nourishes you.

What Sacred Receiving Looks Like

Financial Receiving:

- Fair compensation for your work without apology, diminishment, or constant justification
- Charging premium prices for premium transformation
- Receiving money as energy exchange, not charity you must somehow "deserve"

Support Receiving:

- Hiring help rather than martyring yourself to the altar of "doing it all"
- Accepting assistance without feeling guilty or weak
- Building a team that supports your vision rather than trying to be a one-woman show

Appreciation Receiving:

- Allowing compliments and gratitude to actually land instead of deflecting them
- Celebrating your wins without immediately minimizing them
- Acknowledging your impact without false humility

Rest Receiving:

- Taking breaks without having to "earn" them through exhaustion
- Enjoying leisure without guilt or the need to be productive
- Honoring your body's natural rhythms

Boundaries Receiving:

- Accepting protection and containers for your energy and time
- Receiving the gift of saying no to what depletes you
- Allowing others to respect your limits without taking it personally

When you struggle to receive these essential elements, you disrupt the sacred cycle of sustainable service. You create a one-way flow that inevitably leads to depletion, resentment, and diminished impact.

The Receiving Revolution in Action

Let me share how this played out with one of my clients. A brilliant coach who was killing herself trying to do everything alone. She came to me burned out, resentful, and ready to quit her calling because she couldn't sustain the pace.

We worked on what I called her "sacred receiving practice," intentionally accepting support, delegating tasks, and honoring her need for assistance. We started small: hiring a virtual assistant for basic admin tasks. Then we expanded: bringing on a social media manager, investing in automation, creating systems that supported rather than drained her.

"What surprised me most," she shared six months later, "was how this practice enhanced rather than diminished my leadership. My team felt more valued because I trusted them with meaningful work, and I had exponentially more energy for the transformational work only I could do. My income doubled, my impact tripled, and my joy returned completely."

This is the receiving revolution, gorgeous. When you allow yourself to receive support, compensation, appreciation, and rest, you don't become less powerful, you become sustainably magnificent.

The Magdalene Maverick's Anti-Hustle Approach to Sacred Service

Here is where my rebellious heart gets absolutely lit up: everything I am sharing with you flies directly in the face of hustle culture, even the "spiritual" hustle culture that's infected our sacred work.

The mainstream business world tells us:

- Work harder, longer hours
- Sacrifice everything for success
- Hustle until you collapse
- More is always better
- Rest is for the weak

The spiritual business world often says:

- Serve everyone who asks
- Never say no to someone in need
- Your prices should be "accessible" (code for: undervalue yourself)
- Good healers don't focus on money
- Boundaries are unspiritual

Both are lies designed to keep us depleted, controllable, and ineffective.

The Magdalene Maverick approach says:

- Work smarter from overflow
- Sustain yourself for long-term impact
- Rest as revolutionary act
- Quality over quantity always
- Boundaries as sacred containers
- Premium pricing for premium transformation
- Serving fewer people more deeply
- Building business around your natural rhythms

This is not just different, it is revolutionary. It's a complete rejection of the depletion model that keeps women exhausted and ineffective.

The Connection Marketing Revolution

Instead of chasing followers, posting constantly, or trying to be everywhere online, the Magdalene Maverick focuses on deep connection with aligned souls. This means:

Quality Over Quantity:

- Serving fewer clients more deeply rather than trying to help everyone
- Building genuine relationships instead of broadcasting to the masses
- Creating intimate community rather than large, disconnected audiences

Sustainable Visibility:

- Showing up authentically when you have something valuable to share
- Sharing from overflow, not obligation
- Building your platform around your natural gifts, not forced strategies

Magnetic Attraction:

- Becoming so aligned with your gifts that perfect clients are naturally drawn to you
- Focusing on transformation rather than marketing tactics
- Trusting that the right people will find you when you're clear on your medicine

This approach requires more trust and less hustle, more depth and less breadth, more quality and less quantity. It's the anti-hustle approach that creates sustainable success without sacrificing your soul.

Integration Practices for the Modern Magdalene

To fully embody this revolutionary approach to service, here are practices that will anchor these principles into your daily life and business:

Daily Sovereignty Check-In

Each morning, before you open your computer or check messages, ask yourself:

- What does my energy vessel look like today?
- Am I serving from overflow or approaching depletion?
- What do I need to receive today to maintain my sustainable service?
- How can I honor my boundaries while staying heart-centered?

Weekly Boundary Audit

Every week, review:

- Where did I honor my boundaries this week?
- Where did I slip into depletion-based service?
- What patterns am I noticing?
- How can I strengthen my sacred containers?
- What support do I need to maintain my sustainability?

Monthly Magdalene Attunement

Once a month, create sacred space to connect with Mary Magdalene's energy and ask:

- How am I embodying sustainable service?
- Where am I still buying into depletion myths?
- What wants to shift in my approach to giving and receiving?
- How can I serve more powerfully by serving more sustainably?

Seasonal Service Visioning

Four times a year, envision your service through the lens of sustainability:

- What would my business look like if I truly served from overflow?
- How would my impact change if I maintained my energy vessel for decades?
- What legacy do I want to create through sustainable service?
- How can my boundaries become even more sacred and effective?

A Love Letter from Mary Magdalene on Sacred Service

Mary Magdalene sits in radiant presence, her energy both fierce and infinitely loving, speaking directly to your heart

My Beloved Sister,

I see you there, burning so brightly with desire to serve, to heal, to transform this world through your gifts. I see how deeply you care, how your heart breaks open for the suffering you witness, how you pour yourself out like precious oil, believing this is what love requires.

But listen closely, radiant one: I never served from emptiness. Never.

The patriarchal stories painted me as penitent, diminished, grateful for scraps of redemption. But that was never my truth. I came to the ministry as a woman of means, of resources, of sovereign power. I provided for the mission not from poverty but from abundance, not from depletion but from overflow.

Scripture tells you I provided "from my resources". Do you understand the revolutionary nature of this? I gave from what I had, not from what I didn't have. I served from fullness, not emptiness. I offered from strength, not weakness.

This was not accidental, beloved. This was essential wisdom.

How can light illuminate darkness if it extinguishes itself in the process? How can water quench thirst if the vessel shatters? How can love heal if the lover destroys herself in loving?

You were never meant to be a martyr to your gifts. You were never meant to sacrifice your well-being on the altar of service. You were meant to be a channel for divine abundance that flows through you without diminishing you, that nourishes others without depleting you, that creates more energy than it consumes.

Your boundaries are not obstacles to your service but sacred vessels that give it form and power. Like the alabaster jar that held my precious spikenard, your limits don't constrain your love, they preserve it until the perfect moment for offering.

Your self-care is not separate from your service but its very foundation. Your wholeness is not incidental to your impact but its essential prerequisite. Your sustainability is not a luxury but a responsibility to all those you're here to serve across decades, not just moments.

True service—Magdalene service—multiplies rather than diminishes. It creates abundance rather than scarcity. It fills the giver even as it blesses the receiver. It sustains itself through joy rather than sacrifice.

This is your birthright as my spiritual daughter: to serve powerfully without depleting yourself, to give generously without sacrificing your well-being, to transform lives through the overflow of your wholeness rather than the fragments of your depletion.

The world doesn't need your exhaustion, precious one. It doesn't need your martyrdom or your burnout or your resentful service given from empty vessels.

The world needs your vibrant, sustainable presence, year after year, decade after decade. It needs the gifts that only you can offer in the way only you can offer them, flowing from a vessel that remains full even in its most generous giving.

It needs you to model what sustainable service looks like, what boundaries as love look like, and what receiving as sacred practice looks like. It needs you to show other women that we can serve powerfully without destroying ourselves in the process.

This is how you honor my legacy. Not through sacrifice but through sovereignty, not through depletion but through divine abundance, not through burnout but through sustainable brilliance.

Serve like this, and you serve not just with my blessing but in my true tradition, as a woman who knows that real power flows not from sacrifice but from sovereignty, not from depletion but from divine overflow, not from emptiness but from the inexhaustible abundance of a heart aligned with its sacred purpose.

Go now, beautiful revolutionary, Magdalene Maverick. Serve from your overflow. Create from your abundance. Transform the world through your sustainable presence. And know that in doing so, you carry forward the true Magdalene legacy of powerful, sovereign, sustainable service.

With infinite love and revolutionary recognition of your sacred calling,

—**Mary Magdalene**

"The most radical act of service is not giving until you are empty, yet maintaining your fullness so you can give without end. For a depleted light cannot illuminate the darkness, yet one that burns sustainably can guide generations home."

—***Rose Wilder***

Your Sacred Service Manifesto

I am a Magdalene Maverick, and I serve from overflow, not emptiness.

I honor my boundaries as sacred containers for transformation.

I receive as deeply as I give, knowing both are essential to sustainable service.

I reject the lie that depletion equals devotion.

I embrace the truth that my wholeness is my greatest gift to the world.

I serve fewer people more deeply rather than everyone inadequately.

I trust that my sustainable presence creates greater impact than momentary sacrifice.

I am a vessel of divine abundance, and I serve from that inexhaustible source.

And so it is.

GATEWAY 7

Magnetic Presence—Becoming a Beacon of Divine Light

"She who embodies her full radiance needs not chase the world; the world is drawn to her light."

—*Rose Wilder*

The Irresistible Power of Divine Radiance

Sister, I want you to imagine something that will REVOLUTIONIZE how you show up in your business and the world, and completely obliterate every lie you've been sold about "building your brand" and "growing your following."

Picture a woman walking into a crowded room. She has not announced herself with fanfare. She is not wearing anything particularly spectacular or "on-brand." She has not employed any of the visibility tactics the marketing gurus swear by. She is not even trying to command attention.

And yet, the entire energy of the space shifts. Conversations pause mid-sentence. Eyes are naturally drawn to her presence. There's a magnetic pull that cannot be explained through conventional understanding, that has nothing to do with what she's doing and everything to do with who she is being.

THIS is the power of magnetic presence, and beautiful, it is your divine birthright as a Magdalene Maverick.

In a world OBSESSED with visibility strategies, attention-grabbing tactics, and algorithmic approval, I'm about to share a truth so revolutionary it will flip everything you have been taught about "getting seen" completely upside down:

True magnetism is not created through external strategies. It is revealed through internal embodiment.

Let that land for a moment. Feel how different that is from everything you've been taught.

Consider Mary Magdalene, the woman who continues to magnetize millions two millennia after she walked this earth. Nowhere in scripture do we find her marketing herself or strategizing to build a following. There's no record of her employing tactics to be seen or heard, no mention of her "content calendar" or "engagement strategy."

Yet two thousand years later, her presence continues to magnetize millions across every culture, religion, and generation. Her legacy transcends time not because she mastered external strategies but because she embodied a light so authentic, so powerful, so undeniably REAL that it could not be ignored, then or now.

This is the Magdalene way of magnetic presence. Not the exhausting pursuit of being seen, but the sovereign embodiment of your divine light that naturally draws others to your flame like moths to a bonfire.

The Soul-Crushing Hamster Wheel of Strategic Visibility

I understand the IMMENSE pressure you feel in today's business landscape, gorgeous. The relentless demand to be more visible, more present, more "out there." The algorithm-chasing madness that leaves you feeling like you're constantly performing rather than simply being. The subtle but persistent message that your natural radiance isn't enough, that you need strategies, formulas, and frameworks to be truly seen.

The exhausting dance of posting at the "right" times, using the "right" hashtags, creating the "right" hooks, and saying the "right" things to trigger engagement. The way your stomach drops when a post gets low engagement, or how you second-guess your authentic voice because it doesn't match what's trending.

Sister, I have walked this path myself, caught in the hamster wheel of visibility tactics that left me feeling simultaneously exposed and completely unseen. I followed ALL the expert advice, posting at the "optimal" times, using the "proven" hooks, crafting the "right" content designed to "go viral." I analyzed successful posts like they were ancient hieroglyphs, trying to decode the secret formula for being seen.

I chased engagement metrics while my soul quietly withered under the strain of performative presence. I became a chameleon, constantly adjusting my message to match what seemed to work for others, until I could barely recognize my own voice anymore.

Until the day EVERYTHING changed.

During a particularly intense launch that was supposed to be my "breakthrough moment," I found myself in tears before my computer, about to record yet another strategically crafted video that felt nothing like my authentic voice. The words felt like cardboard in my mouth, the energy was completely forced, and I realized I was performing a version of myself I didn't even like.

In that moment of complete surrender and breakdown, I felt Mary Magdalene's presence with such clarity it took my breath away, and her wisdom flowed through me like liquid gold:

"Stop chasing eyes and start embodying light."

What if, I wondered with both terror and exhilaration, I simply abandoned ALL the strategies and showed up as the fullest, most authentic expression of my divine light?

What if instead of chasing visibility, I focused on deepening my embodiment?

What if I trusted that those who needed my medicine would be naturally drawn to my genuine radiance, without me having to manipulate or manufacture their attention?

It was TERRIFYING. It contradicted everything the business world had taught me about visibility, marketing, and "building a brand." But in my heart, in that deep knowing place that Mary Magdalene had reawakened, I knew it was true.

So I did something completely radical: I deleted the entire launch strategy. I unplugged from social media metrics. I stopped obsessively watching what others in my industry were doing, stopped trying to reverse-engineer their success.

Instead, I devoted my energy to embodying my truth so fully that it radiated from every cell, every word, every interaction.

And something absolutely MIRACULOUS happened.

My business did not collapse without the strategies, it thrived in ways I could never have engineered through tactical manipulation. The right clients began finding me through the most unexpected channels: referrals from people I had never worked with, connections through mutual friends, opportunities that appeared out of seemingly nowhere.

My work deepened exponentially. Over time, my impact expanded beyond what I thought possible. My income increased while my stress decreased. And most importantly, I rediscovered the pure JOY of simply being myself rather than performing a version of myself I thought the world wanted to see.

This is the paradigm-shifting truth about magnetic presence that the marketing world doesn't want you to know: The most powerful client attraction force isn't strategic visibility. It is authentic embodiment.

The Sacred Physics of Divine Magnetism

At the heart of the Magdalene approach to magnetic presence lies a profound spiritual truth that also happens to be a fundamental law of physics: Energy attracts like energy.

Just as a magnet doesn't strain, strategize, or struggle to attract iron (the magnetic force is inherent in the nature of the magnet itself, not in its marketing strategy) your authentic presence doesn't need manipulation or tactics to draw your aligned clients. The magnetism is built into your very essence when you're fully embodying your truth.

This sacred physics operates through several KEY principles that will revolutionize how you approach visibility:

Resonance Over Reach

The conventional approach measures success by how many people you reach: followers, views, impressions, all those vanity metrics that leave you feeling empty even when the numbers look good.

The Magdalene approach measures success by how deeply you resonate with those aligned with your frequency. It's about quality of connection, not quantity of contact.

Mary Magdalene didn't speak to the masses from stages or soapboxes. She did not have a massive following or viral content. But those who resonated with her message were so profoundly transformed that they carried her teachings across continents and centuries.

One soul deeply touched creates infinite ripples. A thousand souls barely moved create nothing but surface waves that quickly disappear.

I discovered this revolutionary truth when I stopped trying to make my message appeal to everyone and instead expressed my most authentic truth about trauma recovery, divine feminine leadership, and anti-hustle business building. My engaged community actually decreased in size, which initially terrified me. But the depth of connection and subsequent client investments and transformations expanded exponentially.

Depth Over Volume

Your magnetic power is not determined by how loudly you broadcast or how frequently you post, but by how deeply you embody your truth. When you express from your depths rather than your surface, you activate a resonant field that naturally attracts those seeking your specific medicine.

It's like the difference between a shallow puddle that makes a lot of splash but has no substance, and a deep well that might seem quiet on the surface but offers life-sustaining nourishment to all who drink from it.

One of my clients transformed her entire practice by focusing on the depth of her embodiment rather than the volume of her content. She reduced her posting frequency by 75%, which felt scary at first, but deepened her daily integration practices, spending time each morning in meditation, somatic presence work, and connecting with her core truth.

Within months, her client inquiries had doubled, and they were coming from people who resonated so deeply with her authentic energy that the sales conversations felt more like recognition ceremonies than negotiations.

Sovereignty Over Strategy

True magnetism flows from your sovereign presence, not your strategic performance. When you stand firmly in your authentic essence without seeking validation, approval, or visibility, you emanate a confidence and groundedness that draws others toward your light like plants reaching for the sun.

This requires the courage to trust your own unique expression, even when it contradicts "best practices," industry norms, or what you see working for others. It means being willing to be misunderstood by many in order to be deeply understood by the few who are truly yours to serve.

Sovereignty means you're not performing for an audience, you're expressing from your authentic center, whether anyone is watching or not.

Embodiment Over Advertisement

Here's where everything shifts: You are not promoting a service; you are radiating a frequency. When you focus on fully embodying your truth rather than advertising it, you become a walking transmission of your medicine rather than a mere describer of it.

This is the difference between talking about transformation and being its living embodiment. Between describing your methodology and radiating the results of your own deep work. Between marketing your services and naturally magnetizing those who recognize the medicine you carry.

When you embody your truth, every conversation becomes a demonstration. Every interaction becomes a transmission. Every moment of authentic presence becomes an invitation for others to remember their own truth.

Divine Alignment Over Manual Targeting

Perhaps most revolutionary of all, the Magdalene approach trusts divine orchestration to bring the right connections at the right time. Instead of exhausting yourself trying to identify and target specific audiences, you focus on clarifying and amplifying your unique frequency, trusting that those who need your medicine will be divinely guided to your flame.

This isn't passive wishful thinking or spiritual bypassing. It's active surrender to a higher intelligence than your strategic planning mind, the same intelligence that grows flowers and moves planets and orchestrates the perfect timing of every meaningful encounter in your life.

From Performance to Presence: The Great Liberation

Bounces with excitement because this changes EVERYTHING.

The journey from strategic performance to magnetic presence requires a fundamental shift in how you show up in your business and life. This isn't about abandoning all external expression, it's about transforming the energy behind that expression from seeking to being, from performing to radiating, from chasing to attracting.

Consider these REVOLUTIONARY shifts that will free you from the exhaustion of performative visibility:

From Strategic Content to Truth Transmission

Instead of: Creating content based on engagement metrics, algorithm preferences, and what you think people want to hear

Shift to: Expressing what feels most alive and true in you in this moment, regardless of how it might be received

I stopped scheduling content to hit "optimal posting times" and forcing myself to create when I had nothing authentic to share. Now I share only when I feel a genuine transmission moving through me, and only in the spaces that feel most aligned, whether that's my private community, a personal conversation, or not at all.

Not only is this infinitely more joyful, but the response is actually stronger because people can feel the authenticity like a living thing. They know when you're speaking from your truth versus when you're performing for their approval.

From Constant Visibility to Sovereign Rhythm

Instead of: Forcing yourself to maintain consistent visibility regardless of your energy, cycles, or inner seasons

Honor: Your natural rhythms of expression and withdrawal, speaking and silence, expansion and contraction

Mary Magdalene knew when to speak and when to remain silent, when to step forward into visibility and when to withdraw into sacred solitude. This rhythmic presence, this dance of revelation and concealment, creates far more magnetic power than exhausting, artificial consistency.

Sometimes your medicine is in the speaking. Sometimes it's in the sacred silence. Both are powerful when they're authentic to your inner rhythm.

From External Validation to Internal Alignment

Instead of: Measuring success through likes, shares, comments, and other people's responses to your expression

Trust: Your inner knowing of what feels aligned, in integrity, and energetically sustainable

This means asking "Does this expression feel true and energizing to me?" rather than "Will this get engagement?" It means posting things that might not be "marketable" but are authentic expressions of your current truth.

From Calculated Persona to Authentic Being

Instead of: Crafting a carefully curated business persona designed to appeal to your "ideal client avatar"

Simply: Be the gloriously imperfect, divinely human, radiantly real YOU in all your multifaceted complexity

Release the exhausting performance of strategic vulnerability that has become so popular in modern marketing, sharing calculated stories designed to create connection rather than sharing from genuine wholeness and authentic expression.

From Chasing Algorithms to Trusting Divine Orchestration

Instead of: Trying to manipulate visibility through tactical approaches and platform gaming

Surrender: To the perfect unfolding of who is meant to find you when, trusting divine timing over forced visibility

This is perhaps the most challenging shift because it requires releasing the illusion of control over who sees your offerings and when. But it's also the most liberating, because it frees you from the exhausting attempt to force what can only flow naturally.

Your Unique Magnetic Signature: The Sacred Art of Being Irresistibly You

Dearest wild-hearted sister,

What if I told you that the very thing you've been trying to fix, polish, or make more "acceptable" is actually your greatest superpower? What if that quirky way you laugh, the intensity of your passion, the gentle wisdom that others rush past, or even the rebellious edge that makes you feel "too much" is precisely what makes you absolutely, undeniably magnetic?

Here's what the hustle culture mavens and generic business coaches don't want you to know: Your authentic magnetic presence isn't something you need to manufacture, perfect, or perform. It's something you already ARE, waiting to be unleashed from beneath the layers of "shoulds" and strategic personas you've been taught to wear.

The Sacred Mathematics of Your Magnetism

Precious rebel, just as no two roses emit exactly the same fragrance, no two Magdalene Mavericks radiate identical magnetic presence. Your particular combination of gifts, wisdom, wounds-turned-wisdom, quirks, passions, and wonder creates a frequency signature that is uniquely yours, and magnetically irresistible to those who resonate with your particular medicine.

This isn't about becoming someone else's version of successful or copying another person's magnetic presence. This is about becoming the most radiant, authentic, unapologetic version of yourself.

Mary Magdalene herself understood this sacred mathematics perfectly. She didn't try to be like the other disciples or dim her intuitive gifts to fit in with the boys' club. She didn't apologize for her deep knowing, her emotional intensity, or her unconventional wisdom. She stood in the fullness of her unique expression, and that authenticity became her greatest teaching tool.

The anti-hustle truth bomb: The world doesn't need another carbon copy of someone else's success formula. The world needs the medicine that only YOU can deliver in the way only YOU can deliver it.

Your Natural Magnetic Expressions

Some women naturally express magnetic presence through:

Fierce, passionate intensity that ignites others' courage—like a bonfire that calls people to gather 'round and remember their own inner flame. If this is you, stop dimming your fire to make others comfortable.

Serene, grounded wisdom that creates calm certainty in chaos—like an ancient oak tree that others seek for shelter and perspective during life's storms. If this is you, stop apologizing for your measured pace or feeling pressure to be more animated.

Playful, vibrant joy that awakens creative possibility—like a child's infectious laughter that reminds everyone that life is meant to be delicious and adventurous. If this is you, stop hiding your lightness behind "serious" business personas.

Deep, compassionate holding that allows sacred vulnerability—like a temple where others can safely unwrap their hearts and examine their deepest truths. If this is you, stop undervaluing the power of your presence.

Clear, incisive truth that cuts through confusion and illusion—like a lighthouse that guides ships safely to shore during the fiercest storms. If this is you, stop softening your clarity to avoid making waves.

Rebellious, paradigm-shifting energy that challenges the status quo—like lightning that illuminates what's been hidden and creates new possibilities. If this is you, stop trying to fit into conventional business boxes.

And countless other authentic expressions that have never been seen before because they are uniquely, brilliantly, irreplaceably YOURS.

There is no "right" way to embody magnetic presence. There is only YOUR way, the authentic expression of your particular medicine that the world has been waiting for.

The Liberation of Letting Go: A Story That May Crack Your Heart Wide Open

Let me share a story that illustrates this beautifully and might help you recognize where you've been hiding your own magnetic signature.

One of my clients, Sarah, was literally drowning in the "shoulds" when she came to me. She was trying to embody a passionate, fiery presence because that's what she saw working for other coaches in her field. She forced herself to do aggressive marketing, showed up with energy that felt like wearing someone else's clothes that were three sizes too small, and wondered why her business felt like pushing a boulder uphill while wearing stilettos.

She was exhausted, resentful, and starting to hate the work she'd once loved. "I feel like a fraud," she confessed. "I watch these other successful coaches being so bold and outspoken, and I try to copy their energy, but it feels completely wrong. Maybe I'm just not cut out for this."

When she finally gave herself permission to drop the performance and express her natural quiet, profound depth, the very quality she'd been trying to "fix," her magnetic presence emerged effortlessly. Her client attraction transformed literally overnight.

"I thought I needed to be louder," she shared with tears streaming down her face, but they were tears of relief, not sadness. "But my natural stillness actually creates a more powerful field of attraction for the clients who truly resonate with my work. They tell me they feel instantly calm and safe in my presence, like they can finally breathe deeply and think clearly for the first time in months."

She discovered what I call the superpower of gentle presence: that soft, unshakeable knowing that draws people in like moths to a steady flame. Not because she was performing magnetism or following someone else's formula, but because she was finally BEING magnetic in her own authentic way.

Her business tripled within six months, but more importantly, she fell in love with her work again. She started looking forward to client sessions instead of dreading them. She began attracting clients who specifically sought out her particular brand of quiet wisdom, clients who had been overwhelmed by the louder voices in the industry and were desperately seeking someone who could offer them sanctuary instead of more stimulation.

The Revolutionary Question That Changes Everything

Here's where we flip the script entirely, beautiful:

The question isn't: "How should I perform to be seen?"

The question is: "What is my natural radiance when I am fully, authentically myself?"

This single shift in perspective is where Mary Magdalene becomes our greatest teacher and guide. She didn't perform holiness for the crowds, she embodied it so completely that it radiated from her very being. She didn't try to fit into the disciples' boys club with their rules and hierarchies, she stood in her own sacred authority with such sovereignty that even they had to recognize her power. She didn't apologize for her deep knowing or try to explain it rationally, she let it guide her every step with unwavering trust.

Your Magnetic Signature Activation

Close your eyes for a moment, gorgeous. I want you to think about a time when you felt most alive, most yourself, most connected to your inner knowing and power. Maybe it was when you were:

- Having a soul-deep conversation that lasted until 3 AM, where you felt completely seen and understood
- Creating something beautiful with your hands, losing track of time in the flow of expression
- Offering comfort to someone in deep need, feeling your natural wisdom pour through you
- Standing up for what you believed in, even when it was unpopular or risky
- Dancing like nobody was watching, completely free and uninhibited
- Solving a complex problem with your unique perspective and approach
- Teaching or sharing something you're passionate about, watching others light up with understanding

What was present in that moment? What qualities were naturally emerging through you? How did your energy feel in your body? What was your voice like? How did you move through space?

That, precious soul, is your magnetic signature trying to speak to you. That's your authentic radiance waiting to be unleashed in your business and life.

Here's Your Sacred Assignment

For the next week, instead of asking "What should I do to be more successful?" ask "What wants to emerge through me today?" Instead of following someone else's content calendar, ask "What truth is alive in me right now?" Instead of posting because you "should," share only when you feel genuinely moved to express.

Trust what comes up. Honor what feels alive. Follow what makes your heart sing and your soul feel spacious. Notice how different this feels from strategic performance.

The Magdalene Maverick Method: Writing Your Own Blueprint

As modern-day Magdalene Mavericks, we are not here to follow someone else's blueprint for success, honey. We're here to write our own. We're here to trust our inner compass so completely that we become walking invitations for others to do the same.

Your magnetic signature isn't something you need to develop, perfect, or create from scratch. It's something you need to remember, uncover, and give yourself permission to express fully. It's been there all along, waiting patiently beneath the layers of conditioning and "shoulds" for you to stop trying to be someone else and start celebrating who you already are.

The most magnetic thing you can do is be so authentically yourself that you give others permission to do the same.

Because here's what I know for certain after years of walking this path and witnessing hundreds of women reclaim their authentic magnetic presence: The world does not need another perfect person following someone else's formula. The world needs another real one. Another brave one. Another woman who trusts her inner knowing so completely that she becomes a beacon of possibility for every other woman who's forgotten how magnificent she truly is.

So tell me, precious rebel, what's your magnetic signature wanting to express today? What aspect of your authentic radiance has been hiding behind strategic performance? What would you dare to share if you knew it would magnetize exactly the right people to your flame?

Remember: You are not here to be like anyone else. You are here to be like YOU. And that, my dear Magdalene Maverick, is the most magnetic force in the universe.

Magdalene Light Embodiment Ceremony: Activating Your Magnetic Presence

Set sacred space with rose petals, candles, and crystalline intention.

This is not just a meditation, gorgeous. It's a complete activation and embodiment of your magnetic presence as Mary Magdalene embodied hers, becoming a beacon of divine light that naturally draws your aligned community without any force or manipulation.

Sacred Intention: To activate and embody your authentic magnetic presence, becoming a beacon of divine light that naturally attracts those who need your specific medicine.

What You Will Need:

- A red candle (representing your magnetic presence and life force)
- Rose oil or rose water (representing Mary Magdalene's essence and heart-centered power)
- A small mirror that you can hold comfortably
- A quiet, sacred space where you won't be interrupted
- Your journal for capturing insights that emerge

The Ceremony

Creating Sacred Space:

Light your red candle with intention, saying: *"I illuminate my divine radiance, just as Mary Magdalene stood unwavering in her authentic light, regardless of who understood or approved."*

Place a drop of rose oil on your heart center, feeling the sacred connection as you say: *"I anoint myself with the essence of Magdalene, who knew her worth beyond all doubt and never dimmed her light to make others comfortable."*

Take three deep breaths, feeling yourself dropping into sacred presence and releasing any performance energy from your day.

The Magdalene Mirror Practice

Sit comfortably before your mirror, holding it at heart level so you can gaze softly into your own eyes without judgment or critique.

Breathe deeply, imagining Mary Magdalene standing behind you, her hands on your shoulders, infusing you with her unwavering confidence and magnetic presence.

Look into your own eyes and speak aloud: *"Mary Magdalene, who stood in her truth when others fled, who embodied her authentic power when it was dangerous to do so, infuse me with your magnetic courage and sovereign presence."*

Continue gazing into your own eyes, allowing any masks or personas to dissolve, until you see the authentic you looking back.

The Radiance Activation

Place your hands on your heart center and close your eyes.

Visualize a rose-gold light beginning to glow from your heart center, warm and pulsing with your unique life force.

Allow this light to slowly expand until it fills your entire chest, then your entire body, warming every cell with authentic presence.

Feel this radiance extending beyond your physical form, creating a luminous field around you that pulses with your unique magnetic signature.

As this field expands, affirm with conviction: *"My authentic presence is magnetic without effort or manipulation. I attract all that is aligned with my highest purpose simply by being fully, radiantly, unapologetically myself."*

The Sovereign Declaration

Open your eyes and gaze into the mirror with the fullness of your activated presence.

Speaking directly to your reflection with unwavering presence and fierce love, declare:

"I am a Magdalene Maverick, embodying my divine light without apology, dimming, or strategic manipulation. I release the exhaustion of seeking visibility through performance and embrace the sustainable power of authentic presence. Like Mary Magdalene, I stand in my truth not to be seen by everyone, but because it is who I am. My magnetic presence flows not from what I do or how I perform, but from who I am when I'm fully myself. I trust divine orchestration to bring those who need my medicine to my flame at the perfect time and in the perfect way. I am seen, I am known, I am recognized by those who are mine to serve, not through my striving but through my being. I radiate rather than chase. I embody rather than perform. I trust rather than control. And so it is."

Sealing the Practice

Anoint your third eye (between your eyebrows) with a drop of rose oil, saying: *"I see clearly with the wisdom of Magdalene."*

Anoint your throat with rose oil, saying: *"I speak my truth with the courage of Magdalene."*

Anoint your heart again, saying: *"I love authentically with the open heart of Magdalene."*

Blow out the candle while saying: *"The external flame extinguishes, but my inner light continues to shine eternally, drawing all that is aligned with my highest purpose through the power of my authentic being. And so it is."*

Integration: Perform this ritual monthly during the full moon, or whenever you feel yourself slipping into the exhaustion of seeking visibility rather than embodying authentic presence. Keep your mirror in your sacred space as a reminder to check in with your authentic self regularly.

Amplifying Your Authentic Radiance: Beyond the Basics

While magnetic presence ultimately flows from authentic being rather than strategic doing, there are powerful practices that can help you amplify your natural radiance and remove the blocks that keep your light hidden:

Identify Your Natural Magnetism Patterns

Reflect deeply on when you feel most effortlessly, authentically yourself:

Energy Mapping:

- What qualities emerge naturally in these moments of authentic expression?
- How does your energy affect others when you're in this natural state?
- What aspects of your presence do people consistently recognize and appreciate?
- When do you receive the most genuine compliments or feedback?

A beloved client of mine discovered that her natural magnetism emerged most powerfully when she was in deep listening mode, a quality she would never have thought to emphasize because it seemed so ordinary and "passive" to her. When she began consciously amplifying this gift rather than trying to be more extroverted and outspoken, her magnetic presence expanded dramatically, and her ideal clients started describing her as "the most powerful healer I've ever worked with."

Map Your Unique Magnetic Signature

Create a comprehensive understanding of your authentic presence by exploring:

- **Your Natural Voice:** How you authentically communicate when you're not performing or trying to sound like someone else
- **Your Energy Signature:** How your presence feels to others when you're being genuine—calming, energizing, clarifying, inspiring, grounding, etc.
- **Your Truth Medicine:** The core wisdom you embody and naturally share when you're not censoring yourself
- **Your Sovereign Boundaries:** What protects and preserves your authentic presence vs. what depletes it
- **Your Divine Expression:** How your unique presence manifests in your work, relationships, and creative expression

Transform Performance to Presence

Honestly assess areas where you're still performing rather than being:

Performance Audit Questions:

- Where do you follow formulas rather than expressing authentically?
- When do you feel drained rather than energized after creating content or having business conversations?
- What "shoulds" govern your visibility rather than inner alignment and authentic impulse?
- Which aspects of your business feel forced versus flowing?

Then create presence-based alternatives:

- Instead of posting on a schedule, I'll share when genuinely moved to express something.
- Instead of crafting perfect captions designed for engagement, I'll speak from my heart about what's actually alive in me.

- Instead of following industry trends, I'll express my unique perspective and trust it to find its right audience.
- Instead of trying to appeal to everyone, I'll speak to those who resonate with my authentic frequency.

Your Personal Magnetic Presence Commitment

Create a sacred commitment to embodying your authentic presence consistently:

"As a Magdalene Maverick, I commit to radiating rather than chasing, to embodying rather than performing, to trusting divine orchestration rather than trying to control outcomes. I will express my truth without dilution or apology, honor my natural rhythms without justification, and trust that my authentic presence will magnetize exactly the right opportunities, connections, and clients at the perfect time. I release the exhaustion of strategic visibility and embrace the sustainability of sovereign presence."

Daily Practices for Radiating Without Seeking

Integrate these simple but revolutionary practices into your daily business rhythm to maintain authentic magnetic presence:

Morning Presence Activation

Before engaging with any external input, emails, social media, news, or even client work, spend 5-10 minutes activating your magnetic presence:

- Stand or sit with your spine tall, shoulders relaxed, feeling your connection to both earth and sky
- Place one hand on your heart and one on your lower belly, connecting with your vital centers
- Take several deep breaths, feeling your authentic power awakening from within
- Affirm: *"I embody my full radiance today, not seeking to be seen but simply being who I am."*

- Visualize yourself moving through your day from this place of sovereign, grounded presence

The Sacred Alignment Check

Before creating any content, having any business conversation, or making any visibility choice, pause and check:

- Am I expressing from authentic embodiment or strategic performance?
- Am I speaking to transmit my truth or to impress and gain approval?
- Does this communication feel like an overflow of my authentic presence or a bid for attention?
- What would I share if I trusted that the right people would find it regardless of how "marketable" it seems?

The Sovereign Gaze Practice

In all business interactions—video calls, networking events, client sessions—practice what I call "the sovereign gaze":

- Maintain gentle but unwavering eye contact that conveys presence rather than performing
- Speak at a measured pace that allows your truth to land rather than rushing to fill silence
- Pause fully between thoughts rather than frantically filling every gap
- Listen from genuine presence rather than planning your next impressive response
- Allow your authentic energy to fill the space rather than contracting to make others comfortable

Energetic Boundary Maintenance

Maintain strong energetic boundaries to protect and preserve your magnetic field:

- Visualize your energy as distinctly yours, vibrant, expansive, but contained within your sovereign field
- Create a protective shield of light that allows your radiance to shine out while preventing absorption of others' energy, expectations, or agendas
- After each interaction, consciously release any energy that does not belong to you
- Regularly cleanse your energetic field through nature, movement, breath work, or whatever feels authentic to you

The Evening Integration Practice

Before ending each day, integrate your experience of magnetic presence:

- Acknowledge moments when you embodied your authentic radiance successfully
- Notice instances where you shifted from performance back to presence
- Release any seeking energy, validation needs, or control attempts that may have arisen
- Affirm: *"My light shines by its very nature, not by my effort. I trust my authentic presence to naturally magnetize all that is aligned with my purpose."*

Standing in Your Full Magnetic Power: The Sovereignty Activation

When you need to fully activate your magnetic presence before significant business events, important conversations, or whenever you feel called to amplify your authentic radiance, this practice will anchor you in unshakeable sovereign presence:

Releasing Performance Energy

Stand with feet shoulder-width apart, feeling your deep connection to the earth beneath you.

Raise your arms to shoulder height, palms facing down toward the ground.

Take a deep breath in, gathering all the performance energy, seeking energy, and strategic manipulation energy in your system.

As you exhale forcefully through your mouth, shake your hands vigorously, visualizing all performance-based energy leaving your body and being absorbed by the earth for transformation.

Repeat three times, declaring with increasing power: *"I release all performance. I release all seeking. I release all manipulation. I release all control. I am free to simply BE."*

The Magdalene Sovereign Stance

Stand tall with feet firmly planted, feeling your connection to both earth and sky.

Place your right hand on your heart and left hand on your lower belly, connecting with your power centers.

Breathe deeply into both hands, feeling your life force awakening.

Visualize Mary Magdalene standing behind you, her hands on your shoulders, infusing you with her unshakeable confidence and magnetic sovereignty.

Feel your spine lengthening, shoulders relaxing, presence expanding in all directions.

Breathe in this empowered posture for seven complete cycles, each breath strengthening your magnetic field.

The Embodied Activation Movement

Begin to move your body in ways that feel authentically powerful. There's no right way, only YOUR way.

Let your body express your authentic presence without choreography or self-consciousness. This might be:

- Gentle swaying that connects you to your feminine flow
- Strong, grounded movements that anchor your power
- Graceful gestures that express your natural elegance
- Bold, expansive movements that claim your space
- Whatever wants to emerge through your unique expression

As you move, visualize your magnetic field expanding around you, pulsing with your authentic life force.

Continue for at least five minutes, allowing the movement to evolve naturally and organically, trusting your body's wisdom completely.

Sealing Your Magnetic Field

Return to your sovereign stance, feet planted, spine tall, hands on heart and belly.

Visualize your expanded magnetic field stabilizing around you like a radiant sphere of authentic presence.

Say with complete embodiment: *"My magnetic presence is activated, stable, and sovereign. I carry this embodied radiance into all my expressions and interactions. I am a beacon of authentic light, and I trust that those who need my medicine will be naturally drawn to my flame."*

This powerful practice creates an unshakeable energetic foundation before client sessions, speaking engagements, video recordings, networking events, or any situation where you want to show up with your full magnetic presence.

The Anti-Hustle Approach to Magnetic Visibility

Here is where my Magdalene Maverick heart gets absolutely electric with excitement: everything I'm sharing with you is the complete antithesis of hustle culture, even the "spiritual" hustle culture that's infected our sacred work with toxic productivity and endless visibility demands.

The Hustle Culture Lies vs. Magdalene Maverick Truth

They say: Post consistently every day to stay relevant

We know: Authentic expression follows natural rhythms, not artificial schedules

They say: You need to be everywhere to be successful

We know: Sovereign presence in aligned spaces creates more impact than scattered visibility

They say: More followers equals more success

We know: Deep resonance with the right people trumps surface connection with the masses

They say: You must hustle and grind to build your platform

We know: Sustainable magnetism flows from embodied presence, not exhausting effort

They say: Follow the proven formulas for viral content

We know: Authentic expression creates lasting connection over momentary attention

The Connection Marketing Revolution

Instead of chasing followers, posting constantly, or trying to be everywhere online, the Magdalene Maverick focuses on deep, authentic connection with aligned souls. This approach is revolutionary because it:

Prioritizes Quality Over Quantity:

- Serving fewer clients more deeply rather than trying to help everyone superficially
- Building genuine relationships instead of broadcasting to faceless masses
- Creating intimate community rather than large, disconnected audiences
- Focusing on transformation rather than transaction

Embraces Sustainable Visibility:

- Showing up authentically when you have something valuable to share, not because you "should"
- Sharing from overflow and inspiration, not obligation and strategy
- Building your platform around your natural gifts and rhythms, not forced tactics
- Honoring your energy cycles rather than maintaining artificial consistency

Trusts Magnetic Attraction:

- Becoming so aligned with your gifts that perfect clients are naturally drawn to you
- Focusing on embodying transformation rather than marketing it
- Trusting that the right people will find you when you are clear on your medicine
- Allowing divine orchestration to bring perfect connections at perfect timing

This approach requires more trust and less hustle, more depth and less breadth, more quality and less quantity. It's the anti-hustle approach that creates sustainable success without sacrificing your soul or your sanity.

Integration Practices for the Modern Magdalene

To fully embody this revolutionary approach to magnetic presence, here are practices that will anchor these principles into your daily life and business:

Daily Sovereignty Check-In

Each morning, before opening your computer or checking messages, connect with your authentic presence:

- How does my magnetic field feel today, expansive or contracted?
- What wants to be expressed through me today?
- Am I moving from authentic inspiration or strategic obligation?
- How can I honor my natural rhythm while staying aligned with my purpose?

Weekly Presence Audit

Every week, honestly review your relationship with visibility and magnetic presence:

- Where did I show up authentically versus performing this week?
- What moments felt most magnetic and alive in my expression?
- Where did I slip into seeking validation or chasing visibility?
- What patterns am I noticing in how I show up?
- How can I deepen my embodiment and authenticity?

Monthly Magdalene Attunement

Once a month, create sacred space to connect with Mary Magdalene's energy and wisdom:

- How am I embodying authentic magnetic presence?
- Where am I still buying into visibility and performance myths?
- What aspect of my authentic radiance wants to emerge more fully?
- How can my presence become an even more powerful transmission of my medicine?

Seasonal Magnetism Visioning

Four times a year, envision your magnetic presence through the lens of sustainability and authenticity:

- What would my business look like if I trusted my natural magnetism completely?
- How would my impact change if I focused on depth over visibility?
- What legacy do I want to create through authentic, sustainable presence?
- How can my magnetic presence serve the collective awakening of feminine power?

A Love Letter from Mary Magdalene on Magnetic Presence

Mary Magdalene sits in radiant, sovereign presence, her energy both fierce and infinitely loving, speaking directly to your heart with the authority of one who has walked this path

My Beloved Magnetic Light-Bearer,

Do you know why they called me apostle to the apostles? Not because I campaigned for the position, networked strategically, or employed visibility tactics to gain recognition. They called me this because the light I embodied could not be denied, ignored, or diminished, even by those who initially refused to believe a woman could carry such profound wisdom.

I did not strategize to be remembered through centuries. I did not calculate how to make my message go viral or build a following. I did not perform my devotion or market my enlightenment. I simply stood so fully in my truth, so completely in my authentic light, so unwaveringly in my sovereign presence, that time itself could not diminish the power of who I was.

This is the magnetic power I offer you now, precious sister—not power that requires constant performance, exhausting visibility tactics, or the soul-crushing pursuit of external validation. This is the power that flows from simply being so authentically, radiantly, unapologetically yourself that those who need your medicine are naturally drawn to your flame like moths to moonlight.

The world will try to convince you that to be seen, you must constantly seek visibility through strategic manipulation. It will sell you formulas and frameworks for attracting others to your work. It will tell you that your natural radiance isn't enough, that you need to be louder, more frequent, more strategic to matter.

But I tell you this truth that burns in my bones: The most magnetic force in existence is unwavering authenticity. The most powerful client attraction strategy is deepened embodiment of your truth. The most effective way to be seen by those who matter is to stop performing for those who don't and simply be the fullest expression of your divine light.

Listen closely, radiant one: I never dimmed my light to make others comfortable. I never apologized for the intensity of my knowing or the depth of my devotion. I never made myself smaller to fit into spaces that were too confined for my expansive spirit. And neither should you.

Your magnetic presence is not something you create through effort, strategy, or manipulation. It is something you reveal through the sacred surrender to your essential nature, a light so powerful it has never needed tactics to shine, wisdom so profound it speaks without seeking to be heard, presence so authentic it magnetizes truth-seekers across time and space.

Stand in this knowing, beloved. Trust that your authentic presence naturally magnetizes all that is aligned with your highest purpose. Release the exhaustion of seeking external validation and embrace the sustainable power of internal alignment.

The world doesn't need another performer, another strategist, another woman exhausting herself trying to be seen by everyone. The world needs your specific frequency, your particular medicine, your unique transmission of divine light that can only come through the vessel of your authentic being.

You are not here to chase visibility, precious sister. You are here to embody such radiant authenticity that visibility finds you. You are here to be so magnificently yourself that you become a living invitation for others to remember their own forgotten radiance.

This is how you honor my legacy, not through imitation but through your own fearless authenticity, not through performance but through presence, not through seeking to be seen but through the courage to be fully, wildly, unapologetically YOU.

Go now, my beautiful revolutionary, my Magdalene Maverick. Trust your light. Embody your truth. Let your authentic presence be the magnetic force that draws your tribe, your clients, your soul family home to the medicine only you can provide.

And know that in doing so, you carry forward the true Magdalene legacy of magnetic presence that transforms the world not through strategy but through the revolutionary act of being authentically, powerfully, magnificently yourself.

With infinite love and eternal recognition of your magnetic radiance,

—Mary Magdalene

Your Magnetic Presence Manifesto

I am a Magdalene Maverick, and I radiate rather than chase.

I embody my authentic truth rather than performing for approval.

I trust divine orchestration rather than forcing visibility.

I honor my natural rhythms rather than artificial consistency.

I focus on depth of connection rather than breadth of reach.

I express from overflow rather than obligation.

I magnetize my aligned community through authentic presence, not strategic manipulation.

I am a beacon of genuine light in a world hungry for authenticity.

My magnetic presence is my birthright, and I claim it fully.

And so it is.

Sacred Integration Questions for Your Journey:

- What would you dare to express if you knew it would magnetize exactly the right people?
- How would you show up differently if you trusted your authentic presence completely?
- What aspects of your true self have you been hiding behind strategic personas?
- Where in your business do you feel most authentically magnetic, and how can you amplify that?
- What would sustainable, soul-aligned visibility look like for your unique expression?

Remember, gorgeous soul: Your magnetic presence is not something you need to create or perfect, it's something you need to uncover and trust. The world is waiting for your specific frequency, your particular medicine, your unique transmission of authentic light.

Stop chasing visibility and start embodying radiance. Stop performing magnetism and start being magnetic. Stop seeking to be seen and start trusting that your authentic light naturally draws those who need your medicine.

You are a Magdalene Maverick, and your time to shine authentically is NOW.

"When a woman stops exhausting herself trying to be seen and simply embodies her full radiance, she activates a magnetic force that transcends algorithms and analytics, for true visibility flows not from seeking eyes but from being so authentically yourself that your light cannot be overlooked."

—Rose Wilder

GATEWAY 8

Your Sacred Invitation— The Magdalene Maverick Revolution Begins NOW

Precious, wild-hearted sister,

Here we are, at the sacred threshold where knowing becomes being, where wisdom transforms into embodied power, where your Magdalene Maverick journey shifts from beautiful theory to revolutionary practice.

Can you feel it? That electric current of possibility running through your veins? That deep recognition in your soul that whispers, "YES, this is MY way"? That fierce inner knowing that you were born for MORE than the exhausting hamster wheel of hustle culture?

Because here's what I know about you, even if we have never met:

You picked up this book because your soul was already calling you toward the Magdalene way. You have been feeling the magnetic pull toward a different model of success, one that honors your cyclical nature, trusts your divine timing, and celebrates your authentic power. You have been yearning for a business approach that feeds your soul instead of depleting it.

And now, having journeyed through these seven sacred gateways, you are standing at the most important crossroads of your entrepreneurial life:

Will you return to the familiar exhaustion of conventional business wisdom, or will you step boldly into your power as a Magdalene Maverick?

The Revolutionary Choice Before You

Sister, I am not going to pretend this choice is easy. The old paradigm is seductive in its certainty. The hustle culture promises that if you just follow the formula, post on schedule, and push harder, success will inevitably follow. It offers the illusion of control in a world that often feels chaotic.

But you and I both know the truth: That path leads to burnout, resentment, and the hollow echo of achievements that never quite fill the soul-deep hunger for authentic expression.

The Magdalene way asks something different of you.

It asks you to trust your inner compass when the world screams that you are going the wrong direction. It asks you to honor your natural rhythms when everyone else is grinding 24/7. It asks you to serve from overflow when others are martyring themselves for their missions.

It asks you to be so authentically, radiantly yourself that you become a walking invitation for others to remember their own magnificence.

And here is what I have discovered in my own journey and witnessed in hundreds of women I have had the privilege to guide: When you make this choice, when you truly commit to the Magdalene path, magic happens that defies conventional business logic.

Your aligned clients begin finding you through the most mysterious channels. Opportunities appear that you never could have strategized. Your income stabilizes and grows in ways that feel sustainable rather than frantic. Your work deepens. Your impact expands. Your joy returns.

But most importantly, you come home to yourself.

You remember who you were before the world told you who you should be.

You reclaim the wild, wise woman who trusts her knowing above all external authorities.

You embody the sacred revolutionary who changes the world simply by being unapologetically, magnificently herself.

The Sacred Sisterhood Waiting for You

Now, I have to tell you something that might surprise you: You are not meant to walk this path alone.

Mary Magdalene herself did not journey in isolation. She was part of a sacred circle, a community of souls who recognized each other's divine light and supported each other's revolutionary work. She understood that transformation happens in relationships, that some truths can only be lived in community with others who share your vision.

This is why I have created something unprecedented, a sacred container for modern Magdalene Mavericks who are ready to revolutionize success through divine love.

Inner Light Collective (ILC)

www.innerlightcollective.org
www.luminaryilc.com

We are not another business program or coaching container. This is a living, breathing community of women who are actively choosing the Magdalene way as a lifestyle, supporting each other as we dismantle old paradigms and birth new models of authentic success.

Inside this sacred space, you will find:

Your Magdalene Maverick Sisters—Women who understand your journey intimately because they are walking it too. No more explaining why you won't follow the latest marketing trend or apologizing for honoring your cyclical nature. Here, your authentic approach to business is not just accepted, it's celebrated.

Revolutionary Professional Alchemy—Not cookie-cutter strategies, instead personalized guidance that honors your unique gifts, natural rhythms, and soul's calling. When you choose to join a dedicated journey, you will be supported should you choose to accept it and take action to design a personal, professional, or ministry model that feels as authentic as your fingerprint and as sustainable as your breath.

Sacred Gatherings and Support—Regular gatherings where you can share your wins, work through challenges, and receive the kind of deep witnessing that transforms both your business and your being. This is not networking, it's soul recognition.

Direct Access to Magdalene Wisdom—Through our live calls, intensive workshops, and sacred ceremonies, you will receive ongoing guidance to help you navigate the challenges and celebrate the victories of your Magdalene Maverick journey.

The Anti-Hustle Business Lab—Where we experiment with radical approaches to client attraction, income generation, and business growth that honor your humanity while creating extraordinary results.

Your Personal Invitation from My Heart to Yours

Beautiful soul, I want to share something deeply personal with you.

When I first began my own Magdalene way journey, I was terrified. Every cell in my body knew it was my truth, yet my mind was about all the ways it could go wrong.

What if I couldn't make money without the aggressive marketing tactics?

What if honoring my cycles meant my business would fail?

What if trusting my inner guidance led me completely off track?

Gasp, what would people say or think about me?

I almost talked myself out of it a dozen times.

But then I remembered Mary Magdalene at the tomb, standing in her knowing even when no one else believed. I remembered her unwavering trust in her inner guidance, even when it contradicted everything the world told her was possible.

And I made the choice that changed everything: I decided to trust my soul's wisdom over my mind's fears.

The path has not always been easy, but it has been ALIVE. It has been authentic. It has been sustainable. And it has been more profitable, both financially and spiritually, than any traditional business model I ever attempted.

More importantly, it has been deeply, profoundly fulfilling. I wake up excited about my work rather than dreading it. I serve from overflow rather than depletion. I attract clients who feel like soul family rather than struggling to convince anyone of my value.

This is what is possible when you stop trying to fit into someone else's business model and start creating one that honors who you actually are.

And this is what I want for you.

Not just the business success, though that will come. Not just the financial freedom, though that's part of it. What I want for you is the profound satisfaction of building something that feeds your soul while serving the world. The deep peace of knowing you are living in complete alignment with your truth. The electric excitement of waking up every day to work that feels like a sacred calling rather than a necessary burden.

The Sacred Question Only You Can Answer

So here are the questions that will determine everything:

Are you ready to stop apologizing for who you are and start celebrating it?

Are you ready to release the exhaustion of trying to be someone else's version of successful and start creating your own?

Are you ready to trust your inner compass so completely that you become a beacon of possibility for every other woman who's forgotten how magnificent she is?

Are you ready to join a sacred sisterhood of women who are actively revolutionizing what success looks like in this world?

If your soul is screaming "YES" (even if your mind is whispering "but what if..."), then I have the most beautiful invitation for you.

Your Gateway to the Magdalene Maverick Way

Stands with radiant, magnetic energy.

The Magdalene Maverick doors are open to well-aligned women who are ready to show up, positively engage, and walk the Magdalene path with sisterhood, support, and sacred guidance.

This is not for everyone. *It is specifically* for women who:

- Are exhausted by conventional business advice that ignores their cyclical nature
- Know they're meant for more than the hustle-and-grind approach to success
- Want to build a business that honors their authentic expression and natural rhythms
- Are ready to trust their inner guidance over external "experts"
- Desire sacred community with other women walking this revolutionary path
- Are committed to doing their inner work while building their outer success

If this sounds like you, I invite you to take the next step.

Visit us at **www.luminaryilc.com** to learn more about our current offerings and discover how you can join our sacred community.

You can also connect with us within our memberships at **https://www.innerlightcollective.org** to experience our online sanctuary where Magdalene Mavericks gather to support each other's revolutionary journeys.

Yet more than visiting a website, I invite you to take the most important step of all:

Trust the whisper of your soul that brought you to this moment.

That inner knowing that this is your path? That's not a coincidence. That is divine guidance.

That magnetic pull toward a different way of doing business? That's your soul calling you home to your authentic power.

That deep recognition that you were born for more than the exhausting hamster wheel of conventional success? That's the truth of who you are asserting itself.

The Revolution Starts with YOU

Beautiful Magdalene Maverick, the world is waiting for your unique medicine. Not the diluted version you think will be more acceptable. Not the strategic version you believe will be more successful. The REAL you—raw, radiant, and revolutionary.

Your authentic success is not just about your personal fulfillment, though that matters immensely. It's about the ripple effect of your embodied wholeness. Every time you choose authenticity over performance, you give others permission to do the same. Every time you honor your natural rhythms, you model sustainability for other women burning out in the grind. Every time you trust your inner guidance, you strengthen the collective feminine wisdom that this world desperately needs.

You are not just building a business. You are participating in a revolution.

A revolution that says women don't have to choose between success and sanity. A revolution that declares our cyclical nature is a superpower, not a liability. A revolution that trusts feminine wisdom as much as masculine strategy.

And every revolution needs its sacred sisterhood.

So I will leave you with this final invitation, this sacred call from my heart to yours:

Don't let fear rob the world of your unique gifts. Don't let doubt convince you that your authentic path isn't valuable. Don't let the familiar exhaustion of old patterns keep you from the revolutionary joy of the Magdalene way.

Step into your power as a Magdalene Maverick. Join the sacred Maverick sisterhood. Let us support you as you birth the business model that honors who you truly are.

The time is now. The invitation is here. The sisterhood is waiting.

Your soul already knows the answer. Trust it.

With infinite love and unwavering belief in your revolutionary potential,

—*Rose Wilder*

The Magdalene Maverick, Founder of ILC
Your sister in the Magdalene Maverick revolution

Your Next Sacred Step

Ready to begin your Magdalene Maverick journey?

- Visit **https://www.luminaryilc.com/home** to sign up for our email list, explore our current offerings, and discover how to work with our team

- Connect at **https://www.innerlightcollective.org** to join our online sanctuary, memberships, Magdalene study groups, and experience our sacred community

- Trust your inner knowing that brought you to this moment—it is your divine guidance calling you home **support@innerlightcollective.org** or **heather@innerlightcollective.org**

The revolution of authentic success begins with your first brave step. We will be here, arms open, ready to support you on every step of the journey.

Welcome home, Magdalene Maverick. Your time is now.

ACKNOWLEDGMENTS

"We rise by lifting others, and I have been lifted by the most extraordinary souls..."
—*Rose Wilder*

My Heart's Foundation

Wade, my beloved—You are the steady ground beneath my wildest dreams and the safe harbor for my storm-tossed heart. Thank you for seeing my light even in the healing moments that I felt that I could not find it myself, for believing in me without question, indulging me completely and enthusiastically, supporting my mission when it felt impossible, and for holding space for both my tears and my triumphs. Your love has been the divine masculine container that supported this work to be born.

My six pack—my babies—You are the reason I fight for a world where authenticity reigns over performance, where truth matters more than popularity, where love is the ultimate rebellion. Watching you grow into your own magnificent selves has taught me that the greatest gift we can give our children is permission to be exactly who they are. You are my greatest teachers and my deepest why.

The Sisters Who Held My Heart

Rosie and Milkface, I love you—Your fierce support, loyalty, and continued unwavering support have been my anchor in the storms. Thank you for seeing me, believing in me, and never letting me forget my worth.

Penny, I love you sister, always there—Through every single season, every struggle, every breakthrough, you have been my constant. Your presence in my life is proof that soul sisters are not born, they are recognized, and I am so grateful to have recognized you.

Natasha—Book Cover Artist, Goddess of Visual Design—Your wisdom and friendship have been gifts beyond measure. Thank you for walking this path alongside me with such grace and authenticity. There are simply no words to express what only you and I have experienced on the journey over the last years. Deepest Gratitude.

Roxanne—In the beginning… there was Roxanne—You were there at the genesis of this dream, believing in possibilities that at moments I had yet to see. Your early faith planted seeds that have grown into this offering to the world.

Heather, the other half—You complete thoughts I have not finished and understand dreams I have not yet spoken. You get the need to hold integrity, always supporting the weaving. Thank you for being my perfect complement, my sacred mirror, my other half in this beautiful dance of sisterhood.

The Temple Pillars: Those Who Hold Sacred Space

To the women who form the sacred architecture of my world, who hold the temple of this work with such devotion and strength:

Ame—Your presence brings such peace and groundedness to everything you touch.

Alishia—Your light illuminates even the darkest corners with hope and possibility.

Rhonda—Your steady wisdom has been a lighthouse in countless storms.

Rachel—Your fierce love and protection have created safety for connection and community to unfold.

Pam—Stay wild, my wild child sister, while also growing into those new priestess panties *wink*

Myriam—Your gentle strength reminds us that power can be both soft and unshakeable.

Bobbie—Your authenticity gives others permission to be real in a world that often demands performance.

Dawn, my twin—We are each other's confidants, holders of secrets and dreams and midnight revelations. You held me and my tears when I truly felt no one could understand the depth of my sorrow and the power in that journey. You are my pizza and chocolate torte friend forever, the one who knows that sometimes healing happens over shared dessert and honest conversation. Thank you for being my soul twin in this lifetime.

Ba Mery—For who you BE, not just what you do. Your essence is a gift to everyone you encounter. Your radiant spirit lights up every room and every heart you touch.

J—Woman, you rock. Your strength, your wisdom, your fierce commitment to being exactly who you are in every moment reminds and inspires me daily.

The Creative Catalysts

All my author sisters on the journey—To the women who dare to put their truth on paper, who transform their wounds into wisdom and their stories into healing medicine for others. You understand the sacred responsibility of sharing our deepest truths, and your courage inspires my own. We are part of an ancient lineage of women who refuse to stay silent.

Jane Astara Ashley—Ah, dearest sister, your words this spring, expressed in divine timing, taught me that some things cannot be rushed, only trusted. Thank you for understanding when I shared that "the good requires and supplies divine timing, which we allowed and honored." Your patience with the sacred unfolding of this work has been a master class in surrendering to divine orchestration rather than forcing human timelines. My sincere prayer is that our journey always continues and abundantly grows.

Learn more:
https://www.luminaryilc.com/
rose@innerlightcollective.org

ABOUT THE AUTHOR
ROSE WILDER

With an alabaster jar in one hand and wildfire in her heart, Rose Wilder stands as an abduction survivor transformed into a prosperity priestess. Walking the Magdalene path with sovereign certainty, she has alchemized her deepest wounds into divine gifts that now illuminate the way for thousands. Her journey from trauma to transcendence was not merely a healing path—it became her soul's revolutionary purpose. As founder of Luminary ILC and a Professional Priestess in the Holy Magdalene Tradition, Rose guides spiritual mavericks who refuse to dim their radiance or discount their worth in a world obsessed with hustle culture.

When you have had to rebuild your entire sense of safety, you develop extraordinary discernment: the ability to recognize what's truly life-giving amidst the noise. This clarity has guided Rose to create multiple thriving businesses, including a healing center, day spa, and professional product line—all while being a Mother to her six beautiful children. She lives with her beloved on her sanctuary farm nestled in the Pacific Northwest mountains.

What distinguishes Rose's approach is her rare integration of seemingly opposite worlds: pragmatic business expertise and mystical Magdalene wisdom. As creator of abundance keys and an energetic Blueprint Mentor, she helps women decondition from conventional success paradigms that exhaust rather than enliven. Her clients learn to anchor their business decisions in their own divine knowing, establishing sacred boundaries while cultivating magnetic abundance that flows from alignment rather than hustle.

Those who work with Rose discover not just a mentor, but a devoted professional holy priestess who holds space for their complete awakening. Through her guidance, women across the globe have reclaimed their divine birthright of prosperity, building businesses that honor both their spiritual gifts and material sovereignty.

Learn More

INNER LIGHT COLLECTIVE—Sacred Sisterhood Where Visionary Entrepreneurs Discover Their Divine Abundance Blueprint

Inner Light Collective Website (www.luminaryilc.com)

Inner Light Collective Sanctuary

Magdalene Maverick Email Sign Up Form

SACRED GIFT

Alabaster Jar Collection—Sacred Magdalene Treasures for the Divine Maverick

"She who knows her worth changes the world with her presence."

The Alabaster Jar collection awaits you, a carefully curated sanctuary of sacred offerings that I have poured my heart and soul into creating. Just as Mary Magdalene approached with her precious spikenard, knowing its inestimable worth and divine purpose, I offer these treasures with absolute certainty in their value to your journey.

- **Sacred Magdalene Meditations**: Experience the transformative power of divine communion through exclusive guided meditations. One created through my own connection to the Magdalene wisdom, and another sacred journey guided by my sister-priestess Natasha. These are not ordinary meditations, dear precious one; they are energetic doorways into the Magdalene temple spaces where your most authentic self awaits.
- **Private Sanctuary Invitation**: Say goodbye to algorithm-driven connections and step into our private Magdalene Maverick Sanctuary, or our Magdalene Maverick journey, all completely off social media. This sacred space is where holy maverick sisters gather to share their wildest visions, deepest questions, and most radiant celebrations, all held in the unshakable container of divine feminine wisdom.

Alright, magnificent one, the magic does not end there! Can you feel the delicious anticipation? Over the next seven months, your inbox will become a portal for divine abundance as I unveil a new sacred treasure each month. Each revelation will arrive like an alabaster jar of precious spikenard, carrying exactly the medicine your maverick heart needs in that moment. Claim your alabaster Jar collection now and begin your eight-month journey of divine abundance revelations. Let these sacred treasures illuminate your path to wild success through divine love.

Access here: **www.luminaryilc.com**

www.RiverRosePress.com

www.ingramcontent.com/pod-product-compliance
Lightning Source LLC
Chambersburg PA
CBHW032253150426
43195CB00008BA/435